NORFOLK CHILDHOOD M
TO BE THERE TO TAL

By

Ronald Ha

NORFOLK CHILDHOOD MEMOIRS- YOU HAD TO BE THERE TO TALK ABOUT IT!

Copyright © July 2018 Ronald Harris

All rights reserved. No part of this book may be reproduced in any form or by any electronic or mechanical means, including information storage and retrieval systems, without permission in writing from the publisher, except by reviewers, who may quote brief passages in a review.

Library of Congress Registration Number: TXu 2-107-472
ISBN: 9781791917166

Printed in the United States of America

TABLE OF CONTENTS

***INTRODUCTION**

***CHAPTER I- "OUR" GENERATION**

***CHAPTER II- WHAT DOES IT MEAN TO REMEMBER?**

***CHAPTER III- A STROLL DOWN MEMORY LANE**

***CHAPTER IV- MY PRICELESS MEMORIES GROWING UP IN HUNTERSVILLE**

***CHAPTER V- SCHOOL DAYS AND CLASS REUNIONS**

***CHAPTER VI- CHURCH STREET**

***CHAPTER VII- WHAT IS 'THE NORFOLK WE REMEMBER'?**

***CHAPTER VIII- WHAT DO WE REMEMBER MOST?**

***CHAPTER IX- "YOU HAD TO BE THERE TO TALK ABOUT IT" QUIZ**

***CHAPTER X- THE GRACE OF GOD**

INTRODUCTION

Our memory is a selection of images, some illusive and printed indelibly on the brain. Each image is like thread, and each thread is woven together to make a needlework of elaborate texture. And the embroidery tells a story, and the story is *OUR PAST*.

In the Judicial system, a *Witness* is a person who sees an event, typically a crime or accident, take place and gives a sworn testimony, we had to be an *"Eyewitness!"* The essence of proclaiming to be Christian is ***being able to provide*** a personal *Witness* of our faith and what God has done for *US*.

Likewise, when you tell someone about a childhood occurrence, you are not telling what you heard but what you personally witnessed. However, as vivid as you attempt to paint a picture of that *'moment'* in time, it might still be arduous for the person with you to share this *'back in our day'* experience. They can merely imagine how it was because *YOU HAD TO BE THERE!* There's no way this book can contain all our childhood memories. I hope it activates some precious, forgotten moment that only *YOU* can tell. ***Enjoy the journey!***

I would be remiss not to give GOD, Lord Jesus Christ, and the Holy Spirit *ALL* the glory and honor for the privilege to just be one of His servants. He has gifted me to be an open book, naked and unashamed, for the sole purpose that **HE**, only, is Glorified. He took a fragmented me and made me whole so that I may use the gift He has given me to encourage or bring a smile to someone else's day. When I was walking through the shadow of death, **HE** showed me that **HE** has always been with me. **HE** is the only reason I can glance back at my life, from childhood to this very moment.

Now, every day when I look back over my shoulder, instead of seeing pain, hurts, disappointments, and sorrows, *ALL* I see is His Grace, Goodness, and Mercy following me *ALL* the days of my life!

CHAPTER I- *'OUR'* GENERATION

To have *"Been There"* you had to be from a unique generation. The first generation of the 20th century, those born between 1901 and 1924, were our parents or grandparents. Next, is the so-called *'Silent Generation'*, children born between 1925-1942 during World War II but were too young to fight. They were a relatively small generation that found itself sandwiched between the war heroes and the prominent and influential Baby Boomer Generation, named for its increased post-WWII birth rate.

Our *Generation* had it much easier than our parents and grandparents. Almost nine months after World War II ended, *"the cry of the baby was heard across the land,"* as this birth explosion was described. More babies were born in 1946 than ever before, 20 percent more than in 1945, the beginning of the so-called *"Baby Boom."* More than four million were birthed annually from 1946 until 1964 when the boom finally tapered. By then, there were 76.4 million *"Baby Boomers"* in the United States. In my family were four brothers and four sisters, all baby boomers. Baraka Obama, the first Black President, is also a *baby boomer*. Our *Generation* was the first generation to grow up with television and live through the civil rights era and the Vietnam War.

Today, the Census Bureau data reveals that **Our Generation** is not only nearly 10% of the African American population, but that we are living longer. Only someone born and raised during our era can equate to these times. It was a time when around the corner seemed a long way and going Downtown seemed like really going somewhere. On our block, seeing only one car on our street was okay. We grew up in homes with one bathroom and only one telephone. We had a living room where we would come together, and we all ate in the kitchen. We did not need for family rooms or extra rooms to dine because when meeting as a family, those two rooms worked just fine. We only had one TV set with maybe, three channels. We had no need for recorded messages because someone was always home. Store-bought snacks were rare because Grandma loved to bake, and nothing could compare to snacks from Betty Crocker's book, or better yet, *from scratch!* We took family trips together, and when we did separate to do things, we knew where the others were without a cell phones. **Remember** when the doctor was a family friend, so we did not need health insurance? **Remember** going to the store or shopping, and when you went to pay, we used our ***own*** money? **Remember** when the cashier had to ***actually count our change?*** We did not have to swipe, slide, or punch in our bill amount!

Our G*ENERATION* recalls *when* penny candy came in a brown paper bag and the *joy* of licking the batter beaters when our mother or Grandma would make cakes. We remember *when* there were two types of sneakers for girls and boys, Keds and PF Flyers, and the only time you wore them at school was for *"Gym"... When* nearly everyone's Mother was at home when we got there...*When* a quarter was a decent allowance and an extra quarter a huge bonus...*When* Saturday morning cartoons were not commercials for action figures.

Our Generation grew up when the music that we played, sang, and danced to, came from a vinyl, holed record called a *45.* The *record player* had a post to keep them in order. Then the records would drop down and play, one at a time. We had our problems back then, just like we do today, but we were always striving, *"keeping on pushing,"* as the last Curtis Mayfield encouraged us. The simple life we lived was so much fun but difficult to translate! How can you explain a game where you just ran and kicked the can? How can you explain why boys would put baseball cards between their bicycle spokes or how for a nickel from a *soda machine,* you could buy little *bottled* Cokes?

Life *"back in the Day,"* seemed so much easier and slower in some ways. And while technology is good, we sure do miss those days, don't we? Nothing stays the same. Time moves on, and so do we, yet we still can relish reminiscing, taking a stroll down *Memory Lane*.

As the late Sam Cooke song *"What A Wonderful World"* goes: "We don't know much about history...Don't know much biology...Don't know much about science books...Don't know much about the French I took." *But We Do Know* that there's nothing like growing up in Norfolk, and *I KNOW* that if you *KNOW* it too, you must also agree, *What A Wonderful Time It To Be!*

CHAPTER II-WHAT DOES IT MEAN *TO REMEMBER?*

This question came to me after reading a Virginian-Pilot article recently regarding the demise of Huntersville, now tagged *"Olde Huntersville."* As I envisioned a community of vacant lots of weeds, trash dumps, and boarded-up homes, I began to remember where the foundation of who I am today was planted.

What is it to **Remember**? Today's technology is way over my head, but the basic concept of a computer is GIGO- Garbage In, Garbage Out, or what you put in it is what comes out of it. As *"Memory"* is the internal storage area (disks of tapes) in every computer that comes with a certain amount of memory, what we **Remember** are also bytes of data stored in our *memory* banks.

Remember brings an image or idea from the past into mind of something or someone from the past. It implies a keeping in *memory* that which may be effortless or unwilled, for instance, *"remembering that day as though it was yesterday."* Is it merely a recollection of information about the past? Or is it **Remembering** the past in such a way that the facts **Remembered** impact our Present? Spiritually speaking, *remembering* would seem to imply that the God, who performed *"Past"* mighty feats for us, is the same God *"Present"* with us, as we *remember* His astounding feats in our lives.

Psychologically to **Remember** means to retain information in our memory or spontaneously recall information stored in our *memory*. What is *Memory*? I'm glad you asked! *Memory* is the ability to recover information about past events or knowledge. It is the power or process of reproducing or recalling what has been learned and retained from experience. Our brain engages in a remarkable reshuffling process to extract what is general and specific about each passing moment. *Memory* is like a photograph, having the ability to remember images accurately. At various times during our lives, we may experience an event that is so joyous or tragic that we recall each moment as if the situation occurred within the last 24 hours. This ability often occurs when an event deeply affects us emotionally, mentally, or physically, *something we all can identify with.* For us to recall or process events and facts like a computer, we must commit them to *memory*.

Forming a *memory* involves encoding, storing, retaining, and recalling information and past experiences. This process of *memory* encoding began when we are born and occurs continuously.

At times, because our *memory* bank reaches its capacity, we must delete some things. Therefore, we have to decide what to detain and put in our *"Recycle Bin."*

Then, there is a time as we age when there is *memory loss* when we cannot *remember* who walked into the room five minutes before, but we can *remember* childhood friends or events from 50 years ago. In addition, there is something called having a *'Photographic memory.'* It is defined as an ability to vividly recall in detail, after a brief time of exposure, without using a *memory* device that aids information retention in the human memory, for example, an old, faded photo of the Booker T. Drive-In. ***The Photo Is Like A Recipe- The Memory of It Like A Finished Dish.***

We Do Not Remember Days; We Remember Moments. Was there ever a time when the first doll baby was born? Was there ever a time when girls did not love dolls, and little boys did not have something to play with, *even if it were popsicle sticks or rocks?*

Girls playing in doll houses making mud pies, and boys playing *'Cowboys and Indians'* and shooting marbles, have been around as long as children. Why? Because it is so amusing and inspiring to *remember* when we were kids on *'cloud nine'* playing with toy animals and six-shooters with caps, playing house, balancing learner's skates, or riding that first bike, ALL BY OURSELVES! I doubt if there is anyone of us who regrets those childhood days of innocent fun!

Memory is more than just a wastebasket of time stuffed with yesterday's trash. Instead, *memory* is a glorious grab bag of our past from which we can, at leisure, pluck bittersweet experiences of *times gone by* and re-live them. Someone said God gave us memory, that we might have roses in December. ***Leftovers, In Their Less Visible Form, Are Called Memories, Stored In The Refrigerator of Our Mind And The Cupboard of Our Hearts.***

CHAPTER III- A STROLL DOWN MEMORY LANE

"MEMORY LANE" or *"HAPPY re-BIRTHDAY"* is defined as a nostalgic path through the remembered past, a walk or trip down a pathway where we spend some time recollecting our yesteryear. When we say that someone is taking a walk or trip down memory lane, we mean that they are talking, writing, or thinking about something that happened to them a long time ago. As we take a stroll down *"MEMORY LANE,"* we talk about the *past,* revisiting places that were important to us in our youth. If we *"jog"* someone's memory, we have divulged something that helped them remember a thought, event, word, phrase, or experience. Every now and then, someone says something, and we think: *"Hmm, I also remember that!"* We feel validated. It acknowledges a kindred or alike connected spirit of the *same* sentiment, the *same* insight, and even the *same* conclusion.

Nostalgia has been defined as a fervent desire to return, in thought, to a time, place, or feeling in our former part of life. For instance, our childhood memories. Nostalgia, a *"phenomenon,"* is an emotional experience more on par with love than, say, fear. It is about us and those close to us; big moments in our life or memorable settings such as the mention of an elementary school teacher, a high school yearbook photo from Modern Arts Studio, a snapshot of the corner of Church Street and Brambleton Avenue, or an antiquated advertisement of up-coming happenings at Bob's Lounge. Experts have discovered that people turn to *nostalgia* when they are trying to avoid something unpleasant or feeling lonely, to counteract their social anxieties. The end result is a stronger sense of belonging. But *nostalgia* isn't just a compensation tool. It is also an energizing emotion. After delving into *nostalgia*, we felt more connected to our friends and motivated to reconnect with them.

When facing uncertain times, the television industry has gambled that *nostalgia* for old familiar shows will give them an edge and a larger viewing audience. In recent years, TV One and BET, for example, have placed a heavy wager on us revisiting once-popular shows, including *"Good Times"* and *"Sanford and Son."* In comparison, Turner Classic Movies (TCM) takes us back to old movies we watched, as kids, on black and white televisions. Even today's most-hyped and top-selling movie, *"Star Wars-The Last Jedi,"* is a throwback to the original supernatural Star Wars movie in the 1970s. And, of course, it is said that music is also a quick way to spark nostalgia. Songs can elicit both positive emotions like, *"I'm So Proud"* by the Impressions, as well as negative emotions, such as *"Strange Fruit"* by Billie Holiday.

Whereas upbeat songs such as *"Shotgun"* and *"My Girl,"* bring out the *"Happy Days"* in us. Slower songs like *"Two Lovers"* by Mary Wells and *"Ooo Baby Baby"* by Smokey Robinson can simultaneously bring happiness and sadness as we reminisce about that first boyfriend or girlfriend. One of my favorite songs, *"What's Going On,"* has both soothing and somber undertones. The essential ingredient in this Marvin Gaye song had a *personal meaning* connected to my service in Vietnam.

Take the group, the Orlons, who, in 1963, had an album titled *"Down Memory Lane."* Only a few of us may remember this smash album, but if we mentioned some of their hits such as *"South Street," "Wah Watusi," "Not Me,"* and *"Mama Didn't Lie,"* you would remember back in the 60s bopping, dancing the night away at a house party, or home with your favorite dance partner, the **Broom!** Meaningful music sends all the good times flooding back: *Finding old music that we used to love is like getting back in touch with an old Friend.*

A **BIRTHDAY** is defined as the anniversary of our born, typically an occasion for celebrating and giving of gifts. On *'That Day,'* we entered this world bare-skinned or in our **Birthday suit** but as we grew older, our *birthday suit* required regular ironing. Through the years, we blew out all these candles on our Birthday cake, but by the time the last one was lit on our 60th Birthday, the first twenty had almost burned out. Blowing out candles is good exercise for the lungs, so they say! Over the years we have heard all the 'getting old **Birthday** jokes, such as, *"Men learned that the most effective way to remember our wife's or significant other's birthday is to forget it just once!"* Who remembers this one!?!

One month visiting her doctor, a retired schoolteacher explained in detail her problems while her doctor listened very patiently. "Now," said the doctor, "You say that you have shooting pains in your neck, aching knees, frequent dizzy spells, and constant nausea. Just for the record, how old are you?" She spoke happily, *"I will be 49 on my next birthday." "Really!'* commented the doctor quietly, *"I see you have slight memory loss, also!"* When we were younger, most of us knew that having a **Birthday** meant having a **Birthday** party, getting treated *specially* for being *good*, presents, cake, and ice cream. When we were younger, **Birthday** parties were where we decided who our *'good friends'* were. When we were younger, **Birthdays** were fun social events that we eagerly anticipated. *So, what happened?* Why is it that as we get older, **Birthdays** become humdrum or a reminder of our lack of importance? I still have trouble wrapping my mind around why people who seemingly have lived a fulfilling life are so eager to put our lives into slow motion, anxiously counting down the days till the **next Birthday.**

The way I perceive it, **Birthdays** should be celebrated at ***all*** ages. To me, saying *"Happy Birthday"* to someone acknowledges of an event that the person had absolutely no control over. I'm not saying that wishing someone a *Happy Birthday* should be done away with or is wrong or bad, because it is always fantastic to recognize someone and make them feel loved. I think saying *"Congratulations!"* takes it one step further.

It implies that we have *'Earned'* this celebration, especially with life so difficult, fighting the seen and unseen battles in this world. With the stress and pressure that we put on ourselves every day, it should be ***commended*** when someone has overcome another 365 days. Imagine it! ***"Congratulations! You have survived getting up at the crack of dawn every day. HAPPY RE-BIRTHDAY!"***

Also, there is a phenomenon called the *New Birth* or *Rebirth*, defined as a period of *'New life.'* What happens as we *Rebirth* ourselves? It can feel like being **Reborn!** What becomes available are intense and ecstatic feelings of revitalization and love, a sense of enthusiasm as our bygone years has seemingly *reincarnated* us.

Our childhood begins anew, and life feels fresh, exciting, and to varying degrees, full of expectations. Old Relationships become the playground for conscious connection and sharing, and we crave to return back to a magical enchantment as we explore *"Back in The Day."*

Rebirth is often a part of the healing process, re-living together, related our childhood memoirs, those miraculous *Rebirths* about what was lost or forgotten, some happy, some sad: For instance, memories of how the delicious aromas of Church Street once satiated our lungs. It gives us a *rebirth* of ourselves, or better yet, of our inner child.

Studies have revealed that each of us has a first memory, but the average age at which those first memories begin until three years of age. Each of us has a personal *'beginning time,'* the first events we recall. Our memories are not only the home of our life story. They hold the key to the essence of who we are, thus, continually rousing a yearning for moments in time we have not yet tapped into.

There is a fifth dimension beyond what is known to humanity. It is a dimension as vast as space and as timeless as infinity. It is the middle ground between light and shadow, science and superstition, and the pit of our fears and the summit of our knowledge. It is the dimension of *Remembering When,* a domain I have dubbed ***"NORFOLK CHILDHOOD MEMOIRS."***

You unlock this door with a key of imagination and enter into another dimension, a dimension of *oldies but goodies*…A dimension of stumbling over photographs that make you laugh as you see happiness and sometimes pain…A dimension of refreshing memories of a time long gone but not forgotten. As you turn the pages, you will cross over into a place and time that *You Had To Be There To Talk About It,* stepping into this dimension as parents, grandmothers, grandfathers, and great-grandparents. Just like that, we are youngsters again, recalling times when we ran tirelessly up and down the streets, climbed, jumped, and danced *ALL* **day**, with no signs of **"Bursitis, Osteoarthritis or Arthritis,** the *Ritis Triplets!* In this dimension, instead of taking our daily prescription drugs, we recall a time when drugs were orange-flavored chewable aspirins, Luden's cherry-flavored cough drops, and Black Draught, only if we had **"The Grip,"**

In this dimension, you will recall when *'Drugs'* were a *good thing*! Our parents *'Drug'* us to Church on Sunday morning, Sunday night, and even on Wednesday nights… I was *'Drug'* to Sunday School, *'Drug'* to Vacation Bible School, and *'Drug'* to the altar for prayer. We were *'Drug'* upstairs when we disobeyed, told a lie, brought home a bad report card, or did not speak to grown-ups with respect. For some of us, being *'Drugged'* is still in our veins and affects our behavior in nearly everything we do say and think, even to this day.

In this dimension, you will find yourself on a typical Saturday morning strolling down Church Street: The beer gardens reeking of stale beer, being restocked with Pabst Blue Ribbon, Regent, and Champale, while the sound of the Sidewinders, Ruth Brown, or Gary Bonds from jukeboxes filled the streets.

You find yourself spellbound, running across our Huntersville legends, *The Showmen*, sporting stylish processes and hanging out at Frankie's Birdland Record Shop…You find yourself perusing the billboards at the Regal, Carver, Lenox, Rio, and Dunbar theatres for coming attractions while breathing in a smorgasbord of delectable odors such as; Fresh peanuts from Regal's Peanut Shop, Mister Davis's piping hot pies, Carolina Restaurant rolls, and fried crabs while being entertained by **"Wild Bill"** doing his *thang*.

In this dimension, there are constant memories of having telephones with party lines, listening to *45* RPM records, Grandma licking Green Stamps, and hoping to get a new hot iron. And who could bear those shrieking metal ice cubes trays with levers?

You find yourself recalling these fun Summer times: Boys playing with cap guns, girls competing to see who the best Hula Hooper, bike riding, and playing sandlot baseball games, **all reviving memories.**

Then there were those visits to the Recreation Center pools or City Beach... Eating Kool-Aid powder...Climaxing a hot, steamy day with a snowball, a pint of High's Ice Cream pineapple sherbet, or enjoying a Wood's Drug Store cherry coke after Sunday School. There is remembrance of priceless times when: It took five minutes for the TV to warm up... Nearly everyone's Mom was home when we got home from school...When a quarter was a decent allowance...When You reached into a muddy gutter for a penny and when it was safe to eat off the ground before you died...Your Mom wore nylons that came in two pieces...All your male teachers wore neckties, and female teachers had their hair done regularly and wore high heels... At the **Filling Station,** You get your windshield cleaned, oil checked, and gas pumped without asking, all for *free*...You didn't pay for air *and* got trading stamps to boot! Laundry detergent had free glasses, dishes, or towels hidden inside the box...Teachers threatened to keep kids back a grade if they failed, and they **Did!** ...No one ever asked where the car keys were because they were always in the car, in the ignition, and the doors were never locked... Being sent to the Principal's office was nothing compared to the fate that awaited us at home... We feared for our lives, but it wasn't because of drive-by shootings, drugs, gangs, etc. Our parents and grandparents were a more significant threat! But we survived because their love was greater than the threat.

"NORFOLK CHILDHOOD MEMOIRS" is a dimension in time where tough decisions were made by *"eeny-meeny-miny-moe"*... And a *"race issue"* meant arguing about who ran the fastest... Catching lightning bugs could cheerfully occupy our entire evening... It wasn't odd to have two or three **'Best Friends."** Baseball cards in the spokes transformed any bike into a motorcycle... Having a weapon in school meant being caught with a slingshot or throwing spitballs, and water balloons were the ultimate weapon, and *'War'* was a card game.

If you can put this book down, when you re-open it, **Wham (!!),** you are back on **Memory Lane,** revisiting fond memories of growing up in Norfolk. **Before long,** you hear of streets you haven't heard of in eons; then **Wham,** there you are, walking through these streets to School, taking a shortcut to the corner store, or chasing down the Mr. Softee ice cream truck on *your* **block** that no longer exist because of something called **re-development.**

As you continue to travel down this *'yellow brick road,'* you might encounter classmates who you celebrated *"May Day"* with at elementary school, then **Wham,** there we are playing *"Red Light,"* two-hand touch football, or looking up in the night sky to see who can find the **Big Dipper** first.

Before long, what seemed minutes, had been hours, and you must run to pick up the grandkids from Day Care, visit the nursing home, and make your doctor's appointments. So, you are back to the senior citizen dimension called **Retirement**, your knees begin to ache on the way up the stairs, take your **meds** and try to recall, *"For the life of me, what did I come into the kitchen for?"*

It Isn't So Much What We Remember As Much As What We Don't Forget! I had been married for over 19 years before I took my family on vacation to visit Norfolk in 2002. It was also the 35th Class Reunion for the Booker T class of 1967. After stopping to see my oldest sister, Celestine, on Holt Street in Tidewater Park, excitedly, I drove to Washington Avenue to visit the few remaining families still living on the block. As we pulled up, I pointed to the house across the street, where I was born and lived for the first nine years. Now it had been torn down and an apartment complex was there. Yet, when I looked at the place where I lived, ***764 Washington Avenue***, I only saw fun, good times playing I-Spy, touch football in the street, baseball in the *"Y-Yard,"* and having bare feet races for bragging rights as to who was the fastest runner on our block.

Next, we turned onto O'Keefe Street and stopped in front of Grandma's house, where I lived until joining the Army at the age of eighteen. All my wife, daughter, and niece observed was a vacant lot of weeds. As we stood in front of ***1415 O'Keefe Street***, they didn't see my Grandmother sitting on her squeaky glider or the little garden she had planted in the front yard, nor did they hear the Mister Softee jingle or the sounds of skaters on Christmas morning gliding to C Avenue. After bumping into a few of the guys I grew up with, whom I barely recognized, I decided we would drive to where my mother had died.

They were bewildered when we parked in front of ***1686 Church Street***, now a weedy empty lot., Yet, while they were scratching their heads, I was focused on where I last saw my mother alive.

By this time, my wife, daughter, and niece were noticeably bored, so we headed back to the Turtle Cay Hotel in Virginia Beach, where we were vacationing. It was apparent they did not see what I saw! Later that evening, while they were at the beach, I asked God what I had just experienced.

God said, "What once you experienced, felt, and touched, I have removed from your past, but what you *Remember* will never fade away or die- *It Is My Special Treasure, Just For You!"*

In July 2017, I returned for the BTW class of 1967 50th Class Reunion and stayed at the Sheraton Hotel in an unfamiliar section of Norfolk called *"Waterside"* (??). After getting settled in and a bite to eat, my wife and I called it a night. Being an early riser, I was up and dressed by 6:30 and decided to take a walk around an area that, as kids, respectively, we called the *"Foot."* Fittingly named because if you dived or waded into the water, the water level could come to your knees, and one step later, it would be over your head. As I began to walk, in the distance, I recognized the steeple of the Catholic Church that toweled over Tidewater Park, so I felt comforted, especially when I saw the Downtown Plaza" sign, even though I did not recall it being at this location. As I ventured down Saint Paul Boulevard, through the glare of the sun, as it began to get sultry, I saw St. John's AME Church, Queen Street Baptist Church, and Young's Park!! Oh, the memories that flashed through my mind! If I had scanned over to the left and seen the old Greyhound Bus station, I would have probably fainted! Suddenly, I felt the hot sun and hurried down Bute Street. When I arrived at Church Street and Brambleton Avenue, I suddenly stopped. As I stood at the intersection, I did a 360-degree turn and saw no resemblance to the hubbub of activity that was so vivid in my mind. I murmured, *"Toto, we're ain't in Kansas anymore!"* I begin the turn back and retrace my steps back to the hotel, but when I looked and saw the street sign again, I thought, *"If I just stay on Church Street, I'll be alright."* Or, as Dorothy would say, *"Stay on the yellow brick road."*

Disorientated as I walked, looking for any clue of my recollection of the Church street I grew up on, I visualized the Metropolitan Drug Store, the Enterprise, and the Lenox Theater, where I watched *"Cotton Comes To Harlem."* Now, there stood Chen Garden and a Laundromat in a strip mall. As I continued down Church Street, the streets appeared shorter and not as wide as I recalled. *Or were my legs just longer now?* While mystified, also, I was aware of my surroundings. After all, this was still Huntersville! Attempting to interchange the *"Present"* with my *"Past"* memories had me sniffing for roasted peanuts and those hot Mr. Davis sweet potato pies. Wow, I thought, *"Am I losing my mind?"* When I arrived at Virginia Beach Boulevard, off to the left, I saw New Calvary Baptist Church, where I grew I up, still on the corner of Wide Street.

After walking by First Calvary Baptist Church, I decided to remain on Wide Street to O'Keefe Street, my destination, only to find that Wide Street came to a dead end. One thing I noticed on this **tour** was that while everything had changed drastically, all the Churches, the pillar of the neighborhood, were still standing. I was reminded of the Bible verse, **"Heaven and earth shall pass away, but My Word shall never pass away."**

Now back on Church Street, finally, I was at Johnson Avenue. After what seemed a long, anticipated walk, I turned the corner onto O'Keefe Street or **"OZ."** As I stood in front of this well-manicured lot of grass, for some reason, I didn't feel the dismay as when I was last at this same spot fifteen years earlier. It was here that God and I had a conversation. I wanted to know why God brought me across town on an early and scorching morning just to stand before an empty lot, *Again!?!*

He said, "What you saw this time gives you more verity of how precious your memories of this place are. You are not insane. Your testimony is not just where you came *from*, but more so *where you are today*, so appreciate your testimony! What do you do when what *was* familiar no longer exist? You remember *when* but do not get stuck in *"What Used To Be."* I am closing that chapter, *Turn To The Next Page!"*

It was eight o'clock, so I rushed down Washington Avenue onto Church Street. When I arrived at Princess Anne Road, I remembered, as a teenager when I wanted to go downtown, I took this shortcut through the grass field at Lott Carey Elementary School. When I got to *Smith Street*, there was no Lott Carey, and the area was now an asphalt parking lot. So, I hurried across Virginia Beach Blvd. Somehow, I reeled through the maze, now called Young's Terrace, passing the gym that was our *Madison Square Garden* for Recreation league basketball playoff games.

Finally, I was back at a familiar place, Brambleton and St. Paul Blvd. When I, now sweating, arrived back at the hotel room, my wife asked where I had been. I panted, *"I Just Took A Little Walk."*

CHAPTER IV- MY PRICELESS MEMORIES GROWING UP IN HUNTERSVILLE

Huntersville, one of Norfolk's oldest and most intact communities remaining from the late 19th century, is unique because it was not planned by a company or commission but developed over time. It is also unique because this small area, located today in the heart of the City of Norfolk, was one of the most cosmopolitan of Norfolk's neighborhoods. It was the only predominantly Black neighborhood to be annexed during the more than 70 years of annexation, consisting of tiny frame houses primarily clustered in the backdrop of Church Street. There was once a botanical and zoological park named Lesner's Park, located between Lexington and Washington Avenues in the middle of the neighborhood. There was also an *"old Burying Ground"* north of the intersection of Church and Goff Streets. Blacks were one of the earliest groups to settle in Huntersville. As a utterly self-sustaining area, Huntersville established the city's first Black newspaper, the Norfolk Journal & Guide. P.B. Young, the owner, inhabited a house that continues to stand on A Avenue.

Former residents of Huntersville included the founding publisher of the New Journal & Guide any many other esteemed professionals who greatly impacted Norfolk, especially during segregation. In 1900, Huntersville had grown 70% in housing and 20% in commercial interests along Church Street. Additionally, the industry had expanded due to the sale of Lesner's Park in 1895 to Regent Brewery.

There was more expansion along the neighborhood's northern boundary, with the industry expanding along the Railroad. Norfolk County also built John T. West School within the borders of Huntersville in 1906, which was located on Bolton Street. The only Black public schools in the city during this era were Booker T. Washington High School and John T. West.

In Huntersville, born and raised at 764 Washington Avenue, was where I spent most of my days. It was the era of *"I-Spy stick em in the eye,"* Six cent Lotta Cola sodas, *'three for a penny'* cookies, those gigantic five cents **Rock and Roll** cookies, the Jump rope game *"Chase the Fox,"* *"Puncha Nella,"* *'Small Smokes'* and **Combination** sandwiches from Toy Sun. Before *"Have It Your Way,"* we enjoyed *'That's A Burger'*... We were entertained by *'Mike the Baboon'* and engaged in friendly *chinny* ball wars after a windy storm... **Before** Rita Water Ice gelatos, we bought snowballs with ice cream at the bottom for a dime from **Miss Chance's Confectionary Store** on Church Street.

When **"*choosing*"** or deciding for games, we would put our foot in a circle, and someone would go foot to foot exclaiming, ***"My momma and your momma were hanging clothes and my momma punched your momma in the nose, what color was the blood?"*** Then we would spell that color, foot by foot, until the only foot left was ***'IT!'***

Remember when we would put a stick on our shoulders and double-dared anyone to knock it off? How many of you guys, after a heavy rain, would race those wooden Popsicle sticks down the streams near the curb in the street? Who was bold enough to go swimming off flooded Goff or Wide Streets or at ***"The Foot?"*** Who remembers those starched shirts from the Chinese Laundry rolled neatly in brown paper? We had one between **Regent Brewery** and ***Harold's Market*** on Church Street. Who recalls the dinging bell and pleasant sight of seeing Mister Davis peddling his bike through the **'*hood'*** selling piping-hot 10-cent apple jacks and sweet potato pies? Remember the ***'Nine O'clock Gun'*** that reminded us it was time to come into the house? Does anyone recall getting up early on Saturday morning to take your **"*good*"** clothes to the One-Hour Martinizing Cleaners, then rushing back before it closed at 5 o'clock sharp, only to see a line out the door that snaked to Wide Street? I went to the one on the corner of Virginia Beach Blvd and Church Street. Only true born and raised folks from the Norfolk area could remember experiencing such a time!

You Had To Be There To Talk About It! We didn't have fast food when growing up, and our meals were cooked slowly in a place called *'At Home!'* My Grandmother cooked every day when she got home from her *'day work'* job in Virginia Beach. We sat together at the kitchen table, and if I ***didn't*** like what she put on my plate, I sat there until I ***did*** like it. Before Visa and Master Cards, we had something called a ***revolving charge card*** that was good only at Sears and Roebuck. If we couldn't afford a charge card, ***Greenberg's*** store would let us to put our groceries **"*on the books.*"** I had a bicycle that I used to deliver the Virginian-Pilot that only had one speed, ***slow***. We did not have a television in our house until I was eleven. It was black-and-white, but Grandma had a piece of ***colored*** plastic to cover the screen. I was thirteen before I tasted my first slice of pizza; it was called a ***"pizza pie."*** When I bit into it, I burned the roof of my mouth. The cheese slid off, plastered itself against my chin and burned that, too. ***It is still the best pizza I have ever had!*** I ***never*** had a telephone in my room. The ***only*** phone in the house was in the living room, and it was a party line. Before you could dial, you had to listen and make sure no one else was not already using the line. And steam irons did not exist yet. Instead, Grandma would sprinkle water on the clothes with an old Royal Crown Cola bottle which had a cork with holes in the cap.

MY FAVORITE GRANDMA MEMORY

My grandmother, Julia Cheeks Towns, was born on January 1, 1900, which, as a kid, I thought was the ***coolest*** thing in the world! I never failed to let it be known when birthdays came up in conversations, even to this day. She was a small, strict, and elegant woman born in Macon, North Carolina, of Indian descent. I just knew her father must have been a chief, evident by her long, silky black hair that bounced as she regally walked through the house or along the narrow streets of segregated Huntersville.

While meek and a woman of few words, the respect she always received spoke volumes. Nothing made me prouder as her grandson than our walks to Harold's corner store, or those trips, during the Easter season, to **Robert Hall Men's Store** in the Downtown Plaza. I will never forget our Sunday morning strolls down brutal Wide Street headed for New Calvary Baptist Church and all the ***"How ya doing, Miss Towns"*** she always received, even from the neighborhood drunks and so-called ***"tough guys!"*** **"Momma,"** as I always called her, raised me from eleven. She was *THE* one ray of light in my youthful days of scarcity of confidence, especially after my mother's death when I was eleven. Since she was not one for much hugging and physical affection, I often doubted her love for me, a love that was made obvious one summer day in 1961. A week before the close of the school year, I was struck by a Broadway Taxi while playing ***I-Spy*** or Hide and Seek for those who did not grow up in Huntersville. Luckily, I had no bones broken, but I hit my head so hard on the concrete that I needed stitches. So, ***Momma*** had to take me periodically for check-ups.

One morning, we arrived at King's Daughter's Clinic early because they didn't give Negroes appointments. We just sat and sat, watching white clients come and go like a revolving door. Even at 12 years old, I knew that white people always came first, but after four hours, I guess ***Mom*** had enough, though you could not tell by her demeanor. Calmly, she walked up to the Receptionist and asked to see her boss. Moments later, this tall, middle-aged white Doctor came out. A tone erupted from ***Mom*** that I had never heard. I would not have believed it was her if I had not heard her in my ears: ***"Me and my grandson were the first ones here and I done seen white folk come and go. I am not going to stand for it! We are here because a taxi driver hit him, and somebody's going to see him right now!"*** By this time, everything had come to a halt; everyone was incredulous that such potency was coming from this frail, sixty-one-year-old Nanny with just a 4th grade education. She came back, yanked me from my seat, and said, ***"Come on, boy, we going to see the doctor. I got clothes to wash!"*** Within half an hour, the Doctor had removed my stitches and re-bandaged my head.

At the bus stop, and as we walked home, not a word was uttered, but this little Black boy was beaming, and I kept echoing silently, She Loves Me! She Loves Me! I will always remember this: ***You never needed an invitation to visit Grandma, and her front door was never locked.***

THE REASON FOR THE CHRISTMAS SEASON

There is a misconception that different seasons occur because the Earth is farther from the Sun and sometimes closer. It makes sense when you are close to the Sun, it should be warm and summery, and when you are far away, it should be icy Winter. But this is not true. The Earth travels around the Sun in an almost perfect circle, so it doesn't change by how far away we are from it. There is even a time when God extends or overlaps seasons that perplexes all things. For example, one December, instead of a white Christmas here in Philly, it was nearly 80 degrees outside. During the same time, it snowed in Las Vegas, where it rarely ever snows.

Suddenly, the animals awakened from hibernating, and flocks of birds headed South for the Winter, made a U-turn, and headed back up North. It has been said that Summertime is the best season with its swimming pools and ice cream cones. Others say Fall with its football games and jewel-colored leaves. Others prefer Spring's thunderstorms and blooming flowers, But there was nothing like the Christmas Season; as children, *any* holiday was alright with us! Especially since the Christmas season meant a prolonged period at home and *No School!*

"*Back to the future*" is a phrase that contradicts itself, an oxymoron. In the movie "***Back To The Future,***" Marty McFly is trapped in the past. He spends most of the time trying to return to 1985, but he is stuck in the 1950s. So, in his struggle to get ***Back to the Future,*** this typical American teenager is accidentally sent back to 1955 in the *time machine* invented by a slightly mad scientist who believes he has discovered the secret of time travel. One night in the deserted parking lot of the local shopping mall, he demonstrates his invention. Marty finds himself transported back 30 years to the days when the *present* shopping mall was a farmer's field, and the adult theater of 1985 was playing a *new* 1955 Ronald Reagan movie. He wanders into town, still wearing his 1985 clothing, and the townsfolk look at his goose-down jacket and ask him why he's wearing a life preserver.

Now, *imagine* you have traveled back in time to the days of your youth, memories of your childhood Christmases coming back to you. You returned to the fond memories of setting up the Christmas tree with wrapped gifts around it and watching Christmas movies in your pajamas as your parents transformed the house with decorations. Christmas was a huge family event!

Some of us spent Christmas Eve with our parent's family or Christmas Day traveling to Grandma's where all the family gathered every Christmas. There was always a plenty of food and gifts, but we, as kids, had **no clue** why we celebrated Christmas for the first five or six years. And we did not think, or care. Caught up in all the excitement of something called *"Christmas,"* we just wanted *Toys!!*

For me, one Christmas stands out. I was fifteen and a freshman at Booker T. Washington High. I earned all A's and B's, making the Honor Roll. *Wow was Grandma proud of me!* At our annual Thanksgiving get-together, I overheard her tell my Uncle Edward that she wanted to get me a bicycle for Christmas as a reward for *"getting good marks"* in school. I was ecstatic! A bike was the ultimate present, something I always yearned for, but I never asked for any *'one'* thing for Christmas. because she had chastised me in the past. For three weeks, I was walking on air in anticipation. When it was Christmas Eve, I could not wait to go to bed!

At the crack of dawn, I bolted from bed and shot downstairs. In the hallway, I stopped in my tracks, *before me was the ugliest bicycle I had ever seen!* It was a bright red and white, freshly painted, used, awkward machine. The look on my face told it all. Noticing my smile turned upside down, she asked if anything was wrong. *"Nothing,"* I lied as I hugged and thanked her. After visiting some friends, I learned they also got new bikes for Christmas. Later that afternoon, *Meathead*, who lived across the street, rang the doorbell to ask Grandma if I could come out and play. Up to then, I had not told anyone I had gotten a bike. So ashamed of that bike I couldn't even bear looking at it. *"Did you get that pretty bicycle for Christmas?"* she asked Oliver, his real name. *"Yes, ma'am,"* he answered, grinning from ear to ear. *"Did Ronnie show you his?"* she inquired proudly. *"No, ma'am, I didn't even know he got one. Can he come out and ride with me?" "Sure! Ronnie, come show Oliver your bike!" "But I don't feel like it, Momma. I'm tired." "Nonsense!"*

When I hauled *"my tank"* outside onto the porch, *Meathead* shouted, *"Hey, that's a cool bike, red and white, just like mine!"* A group of the fellows rode up on their new bikes. Surprisingly, no one ridiculed mine.

Grandma noticed that evening at supper I had returned to my old self. *"This morning, your chin was dragging on the floor. Why?"* Before I could reply, she continued, *"I know why. You were disappointed that your bicycle wasn't brand new, weren't you?"* I shook my head. *"But when your buddies approved, you cheered up because everything was okay then, right?"* I lowered my head again and nodded.

She continued, *"Remember when I told you most kids have parents who work and can provide for them, and you don't? I didn't mean that you couldn't get some of the same things, but that you should not take such things for granted. I meant that! I love you like you were my own son. You are a good, smart, well-behaved boy, and because I do love you, I tried to show you that good things come to good people. This morning when I saw the smile on your face vanish, you hurt me, boy!" "I'm sorry, Momma, I didn't mean to,"* I replied.

"I know you didn't mean it. The point I am making is that gifts from the heart are the best gifts, regardless of the quality or value. It is the thought that counts." I felt so awful that I cried. In retrospect, I understood that she was strengthening me to survive in this world without her. Even to this day, I feel overly blessed to have received the greatest gift of all, her gift of everlasting love. ***Thank You, Grandma!***

Are You Back In Time Yet? Do you see yourself and your family on the floor watching these Christmas classics such as ***"It's A Wonderful Life," "Miracle On 34th Street," "A Christmas Story," "A Holiday Affair,"*** or ***"The Wizard of Oz,"*** timeless shows that were on TV every Christmas season?

Whether the Christmas season began in September until after December 25th, Christmas tunes were one of the best parts of the season, especially on Church Street. There was nothing hipper than listening to Nat King Cole smoothly crooning: ***"Chestnuts roasting on an open fire, Jack Frost nipping at your nose...Yuletide carols being sung by a choir and folks dressed up like Eskimos... Everybody knows a turkey and some mistletoe help to make the season bright. Tiny tots with their eyes all aglow will find it hard to sleep tonight."*** Or The Temptation's melodious ***"Rudolph The Red-Nosed Reindeer."*** Then there was ***"A Charlie Brown Christmas Show,"*** the first television special based on the comic strip ***Peanuts.*** Who remembers the tears swelling up in your eyes when Linus wrapped his blanket around the foot of a pitiful little tree, and all the Peanuts characters would start singing, ***"Christmas time is here, happiness and cheer... Fun for all that children call their favorite time of the year?"***

Now That You Are Back, How Was Your Trip? There was nothing so priceless as seeing the Christmas season through a child's innocent, blissfully excited eyes, licking stamps and Christmas seals on Christmas cards, and standing in the bitter, frigid air, cheering the annual Christmas parade: ***The Macy's Parade was the best!***

If nothing else, the Christmas season was an excellent time to think of everything that has happened within the last year, graceful sharing with each other, and thank God.

The Book of Esther is the *only* book in the Bible that the word **GOD** is not mentioned, but if we read it without this knowledge, we would never notice it. Likewise, *God* is here with us whether we know it or not. The theme of Esther is ***"Who knows? Maybe you are here for just such a time as this."*** A time to look back to our humble beginnings. ***Hallelujah, we made it to 2023!*** God has a plan for your life. There are times when God will ask you to do things that are difficult. Can God accomplish His plans without you? Yes. But He asks you to participate in His plans because it strengthens your faith. We may face uncertainty, failure, fear, and suffering as we try to fulfill God's plans for our lives. But God is with us every step of the way. He is working all things for the good of those who love Him.

The ***Christmas*** season is a beautiful moment to gather with family and friends. Whether we stay home, visit the family, or host other holiday events, it is a excellent time to share, provide support and partake in our journey throughout this year. Sure, tangible gifts are always a part of Christmas, but when I look back, those gifts were not my best or favorite memory. As I pondered this, it got me thinking. It made me wonder what others thought as they looked back on their childhood Christmases.

My takeaway is that ***the immaterial gift of love I received was memorable not because of the gift itself but its meaning.*** It wasn't the price or how many gifts there were under the tree. It was the thought behind the gifts, the person gave the presents and the memories surrounding them. More importantly, Christmas is looking back acknowledging that the real ***Reason For Every Season is Jesus Christ.*** Why is ***"Jesus the Reason for the Season and More?"*** We find in this reason for the season, decorations, Christmas cards, and it is a song that we sing. But what makes this famous saying so much more than a holiday cliche? ***Jesus Christ is the reason for the season*** because He gives hope to the bleak and busy lives of those in darkness and those who have forgotten to slow down and enjoy the presence and love of our Savior. For some, Christmas ushers in the season of the hustle and bustle: There are gifts to buy, trees to trim, Christmas plays to attend, and parties to enjoy. Our wallets feel the stress, and so do we. But for others, there is little joy and hope. So, I challenge you (and myself) to put a little less emphasis on gifts, squeeze our children a little tighter and ***let us spoil them as little more!*** Some may feel like you are scrambling to escape the clutches of darkness due of grief, depression, feelings of worthlessness, discouragement, and more, ***Seek And Rest In Jesus Christ!***

A TYPICAL 'PAPER ROUTE' DAY

Who remembers delivering the morning or evening newspapers growing up in Huntersville? I had the Ledger-Star in the afternoon from 12 to 14 years old and the Virginian-Pilot every morning before school until the 12th grade. My Virginian Pilot route was easy because the morning route was handed down from guys in the neighborhood who either finished high school, went to college, joined the military, or had gotten better jobs. In our community, we had Black newspaper distributors that we met at precise drop-off spots. I had over sixty customers, and other than the Sunday edition, delivering was a breeze. But delivering the Ledger-Star was competitive back in the day; ***timing was everything.*** The earlier you purchased the late edition of the Ledger-Star, the faster you could peddle your papers and not get stuck with leftovers.

At the time, the Ledger-Star sold for a nickel, but you could buy them at three cents a copy from a Black distributor for a whopping two cents profit! In Huntersville, that distributor was Mr. Early. Mr. Early lived on Bolton Street and transported bundles of the Ledger-Star in the back in his classic black 1956 Buick that was always spotless and shiny. It was known by all the kids who rushed and gathered around his car *not* to touch or lean on it! He *always* smoked a Roi-Tan cigar and packed a .38 caliber pistol in full view. ***Nobody messed with Mr. Early!***

Unless I walked to the Ledger-Star building on Brambleton Avenue and arrived by 3:30 pm, the earliest time to purchase newspapers was 4:00 pm at Wide Street and Brambleton Avenue, Mr. Early's first Huntersville stop. The only times I went directly to the main Virginian-Pilot building was when visiting my friend, Butch, Norman Payton, who lived in Young's Park. No matter what I was doing, playing ball, or just hanging out, I stopped, ran home to get my paper route money (60 cents), hurried down O'Keefe Street to Wide Street, through Calvert Park, passing the Journal and Guide to Brambleton Avenue.

The key was to be among the first in line when Mr. Early arrived, and he was never late. Usually, I purchased twenty newspapers unless it was Friday when the eagle flew, then I bought twenty-five. Once I had my newspapers, my first stop was always Queen Lounge, where the sailors, and big spenders, hung out. To me, the big perk of selling newspapers was being able to go inside some of the **'*grown-up spots*!'** Delivering the Ledger-Star was incredibly competitive ***back in the day,*** so you had to be fast and have a game plan because the more newspapers sold, ***the more spending cash you had.***

I would go into every beer garden, shoeshine stand, and barbershop from Brambleton Avenue to Princess Anne Road, and of course, *Carolina's restaurant, Toy Sun, Circle's, and Frisco's.* Some of the proprietors were my regular customers, such as two of the sales associates at *Arthur's Men Shop* and the *Cliff's Hat Shop* owner on Olney Road. My objective was to have sold nearly all my newspapers by the time I got the Princess Anne Road because I knew that Mr. Early's next stop was on Wide Street between Princess Anne Road and Goff Street, his busiest spot.

On my better days, after purchasing another twenty newspapers and hawking them in my neighborhood on Church Street, from Goff Street to the *ABC store* near C Avenue, next to the *Plaza Hotel*. At the end of the day, with tips, I would have made *a dollar!* Mind you; *this was from 1962 to 1964!* In a less than two hours, I *still* had my 60 cents, which I put back in my dresser drawer, and an additional 40 cents. Now I had a whole dollar saved and some spending change to boot. *Talk about a happy camper!*

CHAPTER V- SCHOOL DAYS AND CLASS REUNIONS

'*A DEDICATION TO BOOKER T. WASHINGTON HIGH SCHOOL*'

"Five score and seven years ago, our God brought forth upon in the city of Norfolk Booker T Washington High School: conceived in love, with teachers dedicated to the proposition that Black folk were created equal. We confronted the great battlefield of life and succeeded! When we come back together for our Class reunions, it proves that our alma mater, so conceived and dedicated, endured. Today, we give a testimony and to dedicate a considerable portion of our success to the final resting place for those teachers and mentors who gave their lives and hearts that we might live. It is altogether fitting and proper that we should do this. But, in a larger sense, we cannot dedicate, consecrate, and hallow this ground. Our school friends and caring teachers, living and dead, who struggled in the **"Factory,"** have consecrated it far above our inadequate attempts to add or detract. Today's students may not realize nor long remember what other teachers accomplished, but we, the alumni, can *Never* forget what they did there for us.

It is for us, the living, rather, to be committed to the unfinished work that they who fought so nobly advanced. It is rather for us whenever we gather to be dedicated to the great task remaining before us…From those still with us and the honored dead, we take increased dedication to that cause for which they gave the last full measure of love… We here highly resolve that those that have gone before us shall not have died in vain…That BTW, under God, shall have a new birth of liberty, tremendous labor, and awesome love by our teachers: that the coming generations shall not perish from the earth."

MEMOIRS OF BTW THAT CAN'T BE BOTTLED- THE CLASS OF 1967
Date: Fall - 2030
Time: On An Early Sunday Morning

"Good morning, this is *"Tidewater Slim"* of WRAP Action News. And we are here at the site of the old Washington, I mean Booker T. Washington High School, where in thirty minutes the implosion and demolition of this historical shrine will occur, making room for the anticipated and celebrated Joseph Jordan Education and Community Center. On this usually brisk, damp, overcast Sunday morning, a larger-than-expected crowd has gathered.

If we could move the cameras over just left of Princess Anne Road, there is some commotion as a large cluster of older adults, some with lawn chairs, some using walkers and canes, and even several in wheelchairs. "This is truly amazing! "Sir, what is your name? "John Lee." "Sir, what's going on here?" "What you say? Speak a little louder son all those years as a drummer done pretty near took my hearing. Speak in this ear, my good one." "I said, *WHAT'S GOING ON HERE?!*" "Oh, you mean these here, folks?" "See that there school, Booker T? That school is our heart and many of us are here today because of the love and family we found inside them walls. Spider, come over here and tell this here, Reporter, why you are here this morning, with your walker and all." "Huh? What?" "This here is Ron Harris, who always was shy and not much for words. Tell him about Miss Hagan." *"Oh, Miss Hagan, God bless her soul with her fine self! If she were here, I would plant a big one right on her sweet cheeks!* I cut her English class for the whole semester of my senior year. *I didn't do a term paper or anything!* I just knew I would flunk and go to summer school. I had already decided to join the Army because I wasn't going to embarrass myself going to some summer school. But when I looked at my report card, didn't she give me a *'C'!?!* I never saw her to thank her, but I know she *GAVE* me that 'C' because she truly cared for me."

"Ladies and Gentlemen, I think we have the making of an astounding human-interest story. Mister John Lee, are you trying to tell our viewers that there is something irreplaceable about this school?" *"John Lee, let me at him!"* "Who are you, sir?" "Truman, like the president. Don't you know this was the *only* high school Black folks could attend until the mid-1960's? *Everybody went here!* Our grandparents, mothers and fathers, aunts, and uncles. The walls on every floor were covered with graduation classes going back nearly fifty years! My Grand Pop who served in World War I, and my dad, who served in World War II and Korea, graduated from here.

"Spider, remember Johnnie Johnson?" "Yes, didn't Johnnie drop out in 1967 and die in Nam months later?" "Sure did. I went to his funeral." *"Me too, Ron!* It was such a sad time because Chris Selden died in a car accident after school the year before," John Lee replied. "Sir, hold that thought, we must break for a commercial, but we will be right back. Don't go nowhere."

"To those who are just tuning in, we are at the site of the old Booker T Washington High School, home of the Fightin' Bookers, awaiting school's implosion that will take place in, let me see, in twenty minutes. But there appears to be an even bigger story brewing. A large group of elderly Blacks from all over the country, many donning either maroon and white sweatshirts or **The Norfolk We Remember** T-shirts, have assembled to pay homage to their alum. The group seems to be growing by the minute. I have never seen such loyalty and allegiance!

Mr. John Lee, before we broke for commercials, you were about to relate your experience." *"Oh, Yes! Mister Clarion Editor, come over here! Homey, I haven't seen you in a month of Sundays!!!"* "And what is your name, sir?" "Ron, Ron Odom. Wow! Am I on the air!?! One minute while I fix my tie. Okay. You want to know why I'm here for this event, right? I wouldn't miss this day for the world! Everybody, teachers, and the body student body. I owe this school **BIG** time, you hear me!" "There you have it, ladies and gentlemen, another testimony. Wait a minute, Mr. Odom." *"Huh!"* "Why are you crying?" "I was just looking at where the *'Hungry Steps'* used to be, where many of us sat one time or another. *Thank God,* We have come a long, long way. "While we were away, ladies and gentlemen, the crowd continued to balloon as silver-haired grandmothers and balding grandfathers from as far as California merge for what I can only describe as a phenomenon. If we could move the camera to the parking lot where I was told, the Far East Chinese Restaurant, a favorite lunch spot, was once located. There seems to be a crowd forming a circle. What's happening, Miss?" *"Drusilla, class of 69."* "We just thought it only right that we have a moment of reflection for those that have gone to be with the Lord. Would you mind turning off that camera?" As a somber silence reverberated through the atmosphere, pierced only by an occasional sniffle, the roll call began: Julian Brown, Ralph Wilson, Barbara Whitaker, Bruce "Scope" Harris, John Bright, Chris Selden, Don Wilkins, Johnnie Johnson, Clemel Amlet, Carlos Wilkins, Samuel Ridley, Johnnie Whitten, Connie Jordan, Frank Hines, "Chilly" Wilkins, Roger Dungee, Roxson Blount, Francis Myers, Ulysses, Dianne Edwards, Mister Milbourne, Miss Brickhouse, Bernard "Bread" Ervin, Chris Paige, Frank Hines, Leotis Cain, and Larry Cherry.

"We are now back on the air here at the site of Booker T. Washington High, where there will be an implosion of this historic landmark in just five minutes. While off the air, I learned from Mr. T-Bone that there was another school here at this location until 1975. Is that correct, Mr. T-Bone?"

"Sure was, sonny boy! We called it the "Factory" because that is what it looked like. If you get my drift, there was a whole lot of manufacturing going on in that school, Nothing fancy like this here, school; during the winter, many days, we didn't even dress for gym and wore overcoats to class. But, let me tell you, I wouldn't trade those days for nothing in the world!"

"As we countdown this historic day, move the camera a little. There seems to be another hullabaloo. What's your name, Miss?" *"Rhonda, class of 67."* "Miss Rhonda, what is all the commotion about?" "Mr. Slim, you wouldn't understand. The last year many of us saw one another was at our 50th Class Reunion in 2017, and oh, what a time it was! We did the Bop, Slop, and the Jitterbug. We ate crabs in Barraud Park and just had some good old fun!

It was a thrill seeing folks I ain't see since graduation, like T-Bone over there, Diane Nimmo, Joe Simon, Kathy Stith, Shirley Hill, and *"New York City."* Oh, I meant Cathy Caffee. *Wow, I do not believe it!!* There is Adrienne, our Homecoming Queen, still looking the same! Oh my God, there's Judith and Henry Buck still married after all these years! Where is my blood pressure medicine? Excuse me, sonny, but I have got to get me some hugs and kisses."

"Well, there you have it, hundreds of alums, paying their last respects to what was a home away from home for many. Many trekked from as far as California to say, Booker T. Washington High School, *WE LOVE YOU.*" As the cameras zoomed in, with bowed heads in reverence, there was silence, not a dry eye to be found. The only disruptive clamor heard was *10, 9, 8, 7, 6, 5, 4, 3, 2, 1.*

*HEY, YOU'RE ON THE FRONT ROW!" *

Recently, looking back at my 1967 Yearbook homeroom photo, standing on the first row as a fifteen-year-old freshman at Booker T. High School in 1964, God gave me a revelation. Growing up in Huntersville, from a toddler to a teenager, it was not long before I realized guys, who were once the same size as I, grew wider and taller as we got older. This was particularly obvious playing sports, especially contact sports like football and basketball. Yet I did not see myself as small, but they had grown bigger and stronger.

By the time I was a teenager, I had preferred two-hand football over tackle, and all my shots on the basketball court were from what we now call the *'three-point line.'* A lot had to do with the fact that I was a very picky eater. I was no fond of green vegetables, didn't like any dark turkey or chicken meat, and could not fathom putting a piece of meat with any fat in my mouth. I was all stick and bones, though I did not see myself as such. When I rose from sitting down, I was that kid who had an indentation in my pants where my knees had been. Mind you; this was all hindsight. Strangely, I never saw myself as *"little."*

I was still one of the first dudes to be picked for any sport we played, was never bullied, and even had a few girls that *"liked"* me. Besides, being small for my age had perks, such as still paying the children price at the movies, even at 17 years old, which my tall cousin, Jesse, who was the same age didn't like because it meant I had more money to spend on snacks than he did. Because of low masked self-esteem, growing up, I had this chameleon-like cleverness of disappearing from a crowd without notice and avoiding cameras.

The few school class pictures are the only ones I have from my childhood. One of the highlights of my time at Booker T was when we were rehearsing and marching in on Graduation night. The boys had to line up according to height on one side and the girls on the other side of the auditorium. So, I was standing in the middle of the pack, but before long realized I was the 3rd shortest guy in my graduating class! Talk about being in denial!!

Numbers 13:33 reads, *"There we saw the giants, and we were like grasshoppers in OUR SIGHT, and so we were in their sight."* In the Scripture above, God had already promised His people their land. Still, when they saw the people who occupied the land, they envisaged *themselves* as mere grasshoppers, in *"their own sight,"* or in their mind's eye. They *perceived* others as seeing them as they saw themselves! *That Was Me!* I felt some way until we rehearsed marching down the aisle to the stage.

When I looked across the auditorium, behold, I saw that the *fine* Sandra Vaughn was my *partner* and said to myself, **"Being short ain't half bad!"**

Forty years later, the revelation of re-visiting my 10th grade homeroom class picture is this: The Lord said to me, **"Look, you are on the Front Row. When you unconsciously desired to hide, you couldn't."** Then He reminded me of the Chinese Bamboo plant that starts from a tiny seed. The seed is planted in the dirt and watered, yet very little seems to happen in the first year. Despite constant watering, only a tiny shoot sticks out of the ground.

Finally, during the fifth year, the plant grows 90 feet tall in just six weeks! If the bamboo plant immediately shot up 90 feet in the first year, one strong wind would blow it down. By growing deep before it grows tall, it gains the strength it needs to withstand the force of heavy winds.

I recall attending my first reunion in 1997, the 30th for the class of 1967, and bumping into Cecil Hall, who I have known since 1st grade at John T. West Elementary School. He first said to me was **"Ronald, is that you? Man, you have grown, you used to be so short!"** It's odd how others see our growth outward when we don't.

Like the bamboo tree, stable or long-lasting growth begins *inside* us early in life, yet it is frequently tricky to see that change happening *outwardly*. This is necessary to prepare us for what God has for us, *even in our latter years.* This growth that is developed inside of us cultivates strength of character, faith, and conviction to receive what God has promised us.

There is something amazing about Chinese bamboo and the way it grows. Once you plant it, you need to water it, nurture it, and fertilize it every day. But nothing happens the first year. You do the same thing the next year, and still nothing happens and see no results for four long years! But then what happens on the fifth year is just awesome. One morning you wake up and see a small bamboo sprig, then the next day an even bigger one and in five weeks it has grown up to 90 feet. What do you think, did it do all its growing in the last five weeks, or was it growing for four years? It's obvious that the bamboo was growing underground the whole time without visible evidence, but it was growing. It was developing the solid root system necessary to support the height and weight of the bamboo stalk for a lifetime. The Chinese bamboo reminds us of living a successful life. A lesson that starts with a solid root time: To stand strong, like the bamboo grows and develops its root system, if we desire to achieve success, we need a solid foundation to support those things: our character, values, your attitude. **"Hey, You're On The Front Row!"**

A REUNION- MOMENTS OF THEN AND NOW

"Know from whence you came because if you know from whence you came there is no limit to where you can go." (James Baldwin)

As I anticipated my upcoming 50th Booker T. Washington Class Reunion in July 2017, I began to think about how significant Reunions were. A Reunion is an organized gathering of people who have not been together for a long time. There are also distinct reunions, such as a High School Class Reunion, defined as a gathering of people who graduated from an institution, simultaneously. Even if you didn't like school, you don't want to *miss* the excitement and renewed camaraderie that could result from attending a High School Class Reunion. Consider reunions a nostalgic visit to a time and place that formed an essential portion of our lives. Here are some hilarious reasons why you don't want to miss you Class Reunion:

(1). *It Is Nice To See "The Popular" Classmates Now Living 'Ordinary' Lives.* Now, the *class President* operates a small Eldercare facility; the *Homecoming Queen* works part-time in the Wendy's, the self-proclaimed athletic *"Greatest Of All Time"* or *(G.O.A.T.)* lives in a Rehab Center. Still the *class clown* somehow could fly to the Reunion in a private jet all the way from Hollywood, California! **(2).** *The 10th Class Reunion Is Like High School, Part II.* The same people still try to organize, direct and cheer-lead the group. But by now, everyone else can drink alcohol, so that the *orchestrated* program is more bearable. **(3).** *The 20th Reunion Encourages Interesting Liaisons.* For those still single, divorced, or looking, suddenly the *'Plain Jane'* from Algebra class looks cute, and *'Urkel'* from Gym class has learned to dress without wearing white socks. Classmates have lost hair and gained bellies, so we peep at classmates' name tags to recognize them. We pull out reading glasses and proudly show photos of our grandchildren and great-grandchildren, and the *party is over by 10:00 sharp!* And it was at our 50th Class Reunion we learned why *Spanx* was invented.

Then, there are *Family Reunions*, when many members of our extended families from across the country gather. Sometimes reunions are held regularly, for example, on the same date every year. Traditional *family reunion* activities that include cookouts, evening dinners, *oldie-but-goodies* music, the honorary recognition of elders, community contributions, and educational achievements. Storytelling is another component that brings to life tales of ancestors and their accomplishments. Hours are spent reciting fond treasured childhood memories and life lessons taught by sharing family history factoids and the ties that bind.

Our Family Reunions can be summarized by the OJAYS: *"It's so nice to see all the folks you love together ...Sitting and talking about all the things that's been going down...It's been a long, long time since we had a chance to get together... Nobody knows the next time we see each other, Maybe years and years from now."*

THE DYNAMICS OF YOUR NAME TAG

I am truly amazed when I revisit the memory tour of my childhood in Huntersville. It was a community where everybody knew everyone's *play name* nickname name, and *real name.* Family called me *"Ronnie"* and friends called me either Ronnie or *"Spider."* During my school days, from John T. West through Booker T, from the first grade to graduation, I was *"Ronald."* Many years later, I heard that my graduating class of 1967 was planning a 25th Class Reunion at the Airport Hilton. When I arrived for registration, I was given an itinerary of events and a *NAME TAG* with my photo from my yearbook, that I barely recognized. *I hadn't seen it in 25 years!* While I consider myself to have a pretty good memory, without *NAME TAGS*, I would have been guessing who these folks were all night long. *Thank God for NAME TAGS!!*

So, what is a *NAME TAG?* Typically, it is a temporary piece of paper, permanent plastic, or metal, with a person's name attached to the person's clothing or worn around the neck. Proper etiquette states our *NAME TAGS* should be worn above the pocket on the right side of your shirt, blouse, or suit coat. The quintessential thing to remember is that you want those you meet to make direct eye contact with you and see your name as you shake hands or hug.

Some teachers have discovered that *NAME TAGS* are suitable for the beginning days of school when they try to get to know students' names. What I realized about my *NAME TAG* was getting classmates to remember who I was, which most of them could not do if my *NAME TAG* had flipped over.

Our Class Reunion *NAME TAG* is an information identifier revealing our name and connection to those in our midst, linking decades of fond remembrances. Our Names are markers. They not only identify who we are but also *whose* we are. Isn't it amazing when we hear or read someone's name we knew from childhood, that we often envision their face from *back then*? So, what is so significant about our *name tag*, you ask? We may think of our name as a label that doesn't affect anything, but our reputation speaks volumes and has a profound impact!

At my 50th Class Reunion banquet, another Ronald, his wife, my wife, and I sat at the same dinner table. Ronald and our female classmate sat across from us had off-and-on conversations about people and places that they had in common growing up, but her *NAMETAG* was not visible. Ronald kept whispering in my ear that he thought he knew her, but he did not know from when or where. I believed she knew he didn't remember her but, teasingly, would not tell him her **name**. Finally, after about an hour, she showed him her *NAME TAG*. Talk about a lot of hugging and reminiscing about way *BACK IN THE DAY!*

"WHAT'S IN A NAME"? We usually come across this phrase when folks say names don't matter, that all you need to know is what something is, not what it's named. Often this applies to designer brands or fancy handbags. We say, *"What's in a name, anyway? I can buy the knockoffs way cheaper."* So, the question is, why should we assign so much meaning to a *NAME* In the first place? It has been said that our *NAME* has impacted us from school grades to career choices. For instance, the phenomenon whereby the world's fastest man was *NAMED* Bolt; a TV weather forecaster *NAMED* Amy Freeze; a singer *NAMED* Bill Medley; a golfer *NAMED* Tiger Woods; and a poet *NAMED* William Wordsworth.

Growing up in Huntersville, a girl's name was, *oh,* so important to guys! We would stand in the corner in the cold under the lights at night, and whether we could hold a note or not, we would harmonize, singing: *"What's your NAME? I have seen you before…What's your NAME? May I walk you to your door? What's your NAME? Is it Mary or Sue? What's your NAME? Do I stand a chance with you? It's so hard to find a personality with charms like yours for me…Ooh-ee, Ooh-ee, Ooh-ee."* Then, there is what is called a *"Good Name"* which is our opinion about someone.

For instance, when you hear the name **Red Skelton,** you cannot help but laugh. There is a theory *'Good Name'* is a simple name easy to pronounce and is judged more positively. Statistics have proven that people with simple names in law firms tend to make partners faster. In politics, with the notable exception of former President Barack Obama, fewer syllables generally mean more votes, and people vote more for candidates with simpler names. Also, there is an effect known as the *'cocktail party effect.'* If you are at a cocktail party, there could be 100 people in a room, and you could be in one corner of the room. There is a lot of noise, but if someone at the other corner of the room utters your *Name*, you will hear it. It reminds us of those days when we could be down the block, but when our Mom called our *Name*, we knew she was calling us, even if someone else was on the block with the same *Name!*

Remember, This One Big Caveat: **Wear our Name where it makes the most sense, over your heart, with pride!** In the play Romeo and Juliet, there is the phrase, *"A rose by any other name would smell as sweet,"* in which Juliet argues that it does not matter that Romeo is from her family's rival house, Montague!

After attending several class reunions over the years, I am overwhelmed by how many of my BTW classmates whose pedigree was not a family of professionals. Yet today, many of them are retired doctors, school principals, postal workers, educators, and professionals with Master or PhD degrees. Proudly, I flaunt my *NAME TAG,* amazed I was amid such greatness!

MY BTW 50TH CLASS REUNION EXPERIENCE

During the summer of 2017, as I anticipated my upcoming 50TH Class Reunion, I began to ponder how *SIGNIFICANT* it would be. Such a momentous organized gathering of people who graduated from the same High School at the same time, who have not been together for a long time. Wow, here we are between the ages of 68 to 70 years old in the same place, sharing familiar *"Memories!"* '*SIGNIFICANT*' implies being too closely correlated to be attributed to *chance* or *coincidental*. Classmates, often at the same place and at the same time, never knowing how noteworthy *the moment* was at the time. Memory, on the other hand, is like a yearbook photo or old clippings from the *Clarion* school newspaper, having the ability to recall images with great accuracy. At various times during our lives, we may experience an event that is so joyous or tragic that we remember each moment as if the situation occurred within the last 24 hours. This ability often comes when an event deeply affects us emotionally, mentally, or physically. Something we can only identify with because **You Had To Be There To Talk About It!**

I EXPERIENCED THIS: My wife and I arrived at the Waterside Sheraton, where our 50th class reunion was held. After registration and receiving my photo name tag, we entered The *"Hospitality Room,"* or as I like to call it, *"The Welcome Back Capsule"* because it was like I had stepped into a time machine. There were old photos taped to the walls, presentations on the tables, scrapbooks of previous class reunions, and the *"1967 Yearbook"* pictures. Because we were early, the room was nearly empty, so I grabbed the scrapbooks and began to flip the pages slowly. I was so engrossed that I had forgotten my wife was sitting next to me. When I looked at her, it was as if she knew *"where I was"* and smiled as if she was saying, *"It's okay."* An hour later, we went to prepare for the Spirit of Norfolk Cruise Dinner.

Afterward, when I stopped at the Front Desk of the Sheraton to ask a question, I overheard this woman asking the Receptionist about the BTW Class Reunion. I asked her if she was here for the 50th Reunion, and she said, *'Yes!'* I asked her name, and she pointed to her name tag: **Kathy Stith.** Not only did I remember her, but we were both in Mrs. C.F. Jones's homeroom class! As we gathered at the dock, waiting to board the Spirit of Norfolk, I thanked God for *NAME TAGS!* While some of my classmates I remembered from previous reunions or I had kept in contact with through the years, most of them, I recollected only after reading their *NAME TAGS*. The dynamics of a name and a photo are amazing!

Take **"T-Bone"** for instance. When someone mentions his name in a conversation, they talk about those days at Booker T, but when I heard his name or saw his picture in a scrapbook, I envisioned my first-grade classmate at John T West Elementary School. In 1955.

Similarly, if I posted an old picture of **Mary Jane** candy, on Facebook, soon someone would comment how it was their favorite candy, and someone else they did not like peanut butter. Somebody might remember finding a penny on the ground and dashing to the corner store to purchase a **Mary Jane.** Or someone might have a memory of times when a *'Mary Jane'* eased a hunger pain: ***Every*** memory significant! What I found ***Significant*** during the Spirit of Norfolk Cruise Dinner was this: Even though I did not remember everybody seated at our table for dinner, *our conversations took us back to the same places. We all shared the exact moments!*

The highlight of my stay at the Sheraton was meeting Delores Dunbar in the lobby that Saturday afternoon. She wanted a signed copy of my new book. Though we had never met, her contagious smile and lovely demeanor made my wife, and I feel like we were old acquaintances. Afterward, when I returned to **"The Welcome Back Capsule"** in the hotel, both rooms were jammed and overflowed into the hallway. The first three people I recognized were Steve Charity, Washington **"Ba Bro"** Ruffin, and Lawrence Jones, classmates I had not seen since 1967. We all shook hands, embraced, and had a short conversation, and then we went our separate ways to mingle with other classmates. Sure, these were priceless moments, but somewhat anti-climatic, as if I was anticipating much more. Or was I just acting selfish? I fancied chatting with them for hours, re-living those days at Barraud Park, playing Recreation league football. It was then that I realized how descriptive my old memories were. For instance, I was talking to a classmate, **"Horse-collar"** Sessoms, who I had not seen since we bumped into each other in Korea in 1970 while in the Army.

I began to tell him when and where we partied together, and all he could reply was, *"Wow, you are going way back!"* But he did not remember our encounter. Even in school, it was *cool* to be under the radar. At the Reunion presentation and dinner program held in the Ballroom, when my wife and I instinctively entered, I went to the empty table in the rear of the Ballroom.

As the tables began to become occupied, our table consisted of three of us who worked on the *Clarion* school newspaper at the same time, Ron Odom and John Lee. Also at our table was Cecil Hall, another first-grade classmate, and someone else in my 8th grade homeroom class at Jacox Junior High School, Bernadette. She knew my name from school, but only after me naming every student in our homeroom class, as well as our homeroom teacher's name, did she REMEMBER ME. As I scanned the Ballroom, it was uncanny how the ones who hung together back in school were still hanging together. It may have been just my observation, but it reminded me of a social caste system until I mentioned it to someone who concurred with me only applied the term *"bourgeoisie."* I guess some things do not change, but nothing would *impede this once-in-a- lifetime* 50th Year Reunion.

After pausing for a solemn moment to pay homage to our decreased classmates, we intermixed with Booker T alums from as far back as 1962, and graduates from Norcom, our high school nemesis. Grandmas and Pop-Pops danced until the music stopped. Camera phones flashed throughout the night, accumulating remembrances that will never be duplicated, as laughter saturated the Ballroom and reverberated throughout the Waterside Sheraton. If there was one takeaway from the Reunion that I found profound, it was a conversation I had with Jean Pittman and Eugenia Holley while we were in the buffet line getting our dinner.

Jean Pittman, who I had not seen since graduating in 1967, and who was also in my homeroom class, came up to me and introduced herself to me, and began to tell me she enjoyed my Facebook post on *"The Norfolk We Remember."* She asked me if I remembered her. Lightheartedly, flirtatiously, I replied, *"Yep, ever since you lived on Fremont Street!"* Her responding pleasant facial expression told it all.

Standing right behind me, Eugenia began telling me how she left Booker T after her first year and relocated, but that she *did* graduate from Jacox Junior High School. Likewise, she asked me if I remembered her. *"Of Course!"* Surprised, she said, *"Really,"* as if I was appeasing her. Then I said, *"Of course I do! You were a majorette, right!?!"* and smiled at her. She had the same expression on her face that I saw on Jean's face.

When We Remember Or Hear A Familiar Name, It Does Not Remind Us Of The Last Time We Saw Them But The First Time. We All Unconsciously Desire To Be Remembered! It Is Just Something About Knowing Someone From "BACK THEN" ... BEFORE They Graduated From School... BEFORE All the College Degrees and Titles... BEFORE They Got Married ... BEFORE They Had Children ... BEFORE That First Gray Strand Of Hair! **MAY WE FOREVER REMEMBER AND PRAY FOR EACH OTHER!

CHAPTER VI- *"CHURCH STREET"*

Our Norfolk memoirs cannot be told without the mention of the Church Street area where we grew up. Where before the building of housing projects were built in the community, Church Street was an area that was the heart of the Black business district and Norfolk's Black population. As most neighborhoods of Norfolk officially became part of the city during the early 1900s, the era between the 1940s and the 1960s helped the Norfolk Black population to move and live in other parts of the city, other than the Downtown sections. Due to the concept of the Norfolk Housing Authority's construction of housing projects, many Black neighborhoods along Church Street were demolished as *"we moved on up to the east side, to a deluxe apartment in the sky. We finally got a piece of the pie!"*

I have no idea how Church Street was named, but the fact that the first Church, Saint Paul's Episcopal Church, in Norfolk, was built there works for me. Church Street was Norfolk's Harlem, its mecca, Uptown. Church Street went down from *'The Foot,'* I mean the Elizabeth River, north through the heart of Norfolk. Tagged *"The Harlem of the South,"* Church Street was that one-of-a-kind corridor that if you drove or rode the bus down, you were doing yourself a disservice- *YOU HAD TO WALK IT!* I can still recall, as a kid, enjoying my aunts and uncles talking about all the Good Times spent *'juking and jiving'* at Russell's Grill and the Eureka Lodge. It was stated that the city founders killed Church Street and that the Redevelopment and Housing Authority buried it, *but not our memories!*

By the mid-1970s, due to integration, nearly all of the boutiques and professional offices had moved from Church Street to Granby Street, the nearby Downtown Plaza Shopping Center, the Greater Norfolk Plaza office building, or elsewhere. Left behind was an assortment of pawn shops, barber and beauty shops, and clothing and furniture stores catering to those on the edges of society.

In 2017, when visiting Church Street, I observed a dissimilarity between **Today's** Church Street and **Yesteryear's** Church Street. In the old Superman comic books, it is akin to the **Bizarro World**, also known as Htrae, which is "Earth" spelled backward. It was a fictional planet where everything was different and the opposite of how things are on Earth. Sometimes, *I ponder what was lost.* There is still a Church Street with some businesses, but today, it is a fast-moving strip with gas stations, take-out eateries, and new and improved houses. Nowadays, there is very little foot traffic, nothing like the hustle and bustle I remember when I lived on Church Street.

Obviously, *'OUR'* Church Street doesn't exist anymore, but we *CAN* take a memory excursion down Church Street, the fashionable *"Main Street"* of Norfolk's black community! Do you remember when: Soroko's Market was jam-packed on Saturday mornings, and we had a choice of the Carver, Dunbar, Regal, Rio, or Lenox movie theatres to choose from on Saturdays or after Church on Sundays? Who remembers the Booker T, now called the Attucks Theater, a prominent landmark on Church Street?

To this day, the Attucks still stands as a rare example of an early motion theater, financed by two black financial institutions, the Brown Savings Bank and Tidewater Trust Company, designed and built exclusively by Blacks. Who recalls rushing to Virginia Pharmacy or Arthur's Drugstore (formerly the Rio theatre) to pick up a prescription or to place one? Was there a more incredible thrill than scanning the variety of ageless photography outside the *Modern Arts Photo Studio*, looking for a familiar face?

Can you still envision the *Plaza Hotel* on Church Street, owned by the late Bonnie McEachin, *"The Queen of Church Street,"* where the Black entertainers, who headlined in Harlem, came to stay and perform in Norfolk? As a kid, who could ever forget *Daddy Grace*, who I thought was the wealthiest man in the world? Everybody knew Daddy Grace and The United House of Prayer For All People on Church Street! These were the best of days on Church Street! Please, don't believe me! Just ask anyone who grew up during this time because *YOU HAD TO BE THERE TO TALK ABOUT IT!*

*THE "CHURCH STREET SOUND" *

"What Goes Around Comes Around" does not just mean records on a turntable. Those who live and breathe audio swear by the sound quality of vinyl records over CDs and MP3s, and the younger generation, is starting to see the light. Vinyl sales continue to increase each year as CD sales drop, which means that more and more young people are borrowing albums from their parents or buying their own, while those who grew up with vinyl records, like us, are perhaps dusting off our cherished collections.

Do you still remember buying your first *45* or dropping your first nickel in the jukebox? Who recalls moving from apartment to apartment or breaking up with that boyfriend or girlfriend? When you left, you **had** to take your record albums with you! Nothing can compare to listening to an oldie like *"Love Supreme,"* with the meditative quality of vinyl's warm and dusty crackle.

We grew up in the 40s, 50s, and 60s when Doo-Wop was at its peak. Over a half-a-century later, we still enjoy listening to Doo-Wop and many other styles of music simply described as *Good songs, Good memories, and Good sounds*.

It's a period where we can step back in time and relive old memories and where we were when these classic records were playing. It covers our three favorite decades, the 40's, 50's, and 60's, when the golden age of vinyl records was at its peak. So, if you are truly ready to turn back the clock and relive some excellent vinyl record memories, grab your favorite beverage, and pull up a chair: *This could take a while!* So, please close your eyes and take a trip down Memory Lane. A place and time when groovy 45s and LP albums were a part of life no one in today's *digital world* could fully appreciate. We cannot do away with all our vinyl 45s or LPs because they are *old friends.* But we can *do the right thing* by plugging in our record player and showing them, some love back.

Detroit had its Motown, and Norfolk, back in the day, had the *"Church Street Sound."* Like Harlem, we were a community that produced its own culture and rich history, leaving its imprint on the world through music. We had homegrown talents such as: The Anglos, Charlie McClendon & the Magnificents, Little Ida Sands (Norfolk's Queen of Song), Barbara Stant, Lenis Guess, Jimmy Soul, The Positive Sounds, Flip Flop Stevens, The Showmen (formerly the Humdingers), Gary U.S. Bonds, and the Idettes. No sound emulates the Norfolk Sound more than *The Church Street Five,* a house band that backed some legendary vocalists like Gary US Bond's *"Quarter to Three"* and Jimmy Soul's #1 hit *"If You Wanna Be Happy."*

The ***Church Street Five*** group was dubbed by drummer Emmitt Shields, who played in the House of Prayer at the intersection of Church Street and Princess Anne Road. The group, a significant influence on the sound of music, had a sound that bands and labels all over the world tried to copy. I would be remiss not to mention such homegrown legends as Ella Fitzgerald, Pearl Bailey, Ruth Brown, and Huntersville's own Gordon Banks, who played guitar for The Showmen as a teenager.

Remember when Daddy Jack Holmes woke us up with music and the time? In the age of the ***WRAP AM 850*** and the record player, we had Disc Jockeys such as Leola Dyson, Bob King, Dave Riddick, and Frank ***"King Hotdog"*** Halison. They were DJs with personalities who played the music we loved. But more than that, they kept us up on the latest gossip and all the tidbits of info that touched our meager lives and made us feel better, a time when ***"Record Stops"*** were a pillar in our communities.

In Huntersville, we had Nimrod's and Frankie's Birdland Record Shops. Across the street was the House of Process, where performers would get their hair conked. After hearing the latest hit tune, did you rush down to Nimrod's or Birdland to buy the 45? Where we went for the latest and most popular records that we just had to have, either for our collection or that cellar, house, or rent party. It was a hub where you might see or run into anybody, even local celebrities!

Later that night, we went out to the club, where Bob Fields was spinning the records and set the dance floor on fire. Also, it was a joy to party at **'*Church Street Sound*'** local concerts by homegrown artists at spots like ***Longshoreman's Hall, Seaview Beach,*** or ***Sunset Lake Park.***

There was once a building at 408 W. Princess Anne Road in Norfolk, purchased in 1959 by a record store owner named Frank Guida, who used the space to record the works of local singers and musicians, such as Gary U.S. Bonds, Gene Barge and Jimmy Soul. Numerous hits were cut there during the early '60s, including U.S. Bonds' ***"New Orleans"*** and ***"Quarter to Three,"*** and Jimmy Soul's exotic calypso rock 'n' roll tunes, ***"If You Wanna Be Happy"*** and ***"Twisting Matilda."***

A ***"Walk of Fame"*** plaque honoring the achievements of Frank Guida and his sound factory rests somewhere on Granby Street, where one of his record stores stood. But there is no marker or sign near this driveway where the music first started at 408 W. Princess Anne Road.

*MY BEST SATURDAY- A TREK DOWN CHURCH STREET *

After returning from my morning Virginian-Pilot paper route and parking my shopping cart, the aroma of Grandma's homemade biscuits and Gwaltney sausages smacked me in the face as I entered the house. After tugging some hot water upstairs to wash up, brushing my teeth with Arm and Hammer baking soda, chopping wood for the week, and filling the coal bin in the kitchen next to the stove, I grabbed my Virginian-Pilot profits. By 10 am, even at 15 years old, I *still* had to tell Grandma where I was going before hitting the streets. After telling Grandma where I was going, I shot out the door and turned onto Johnson Avenue towards Church Street, **making sure** to take a peep to see if Sheila Johnson was on her porch or in her backyard. She had my nose so wide open I just *knew* they had named the street after her! At the corner, I would peep in Carolina Restaurant to see who was there. Usually, the windows would be steamed up, so I would peep thru the window. If none of the fellows was there, I headed downtown, waving at **Big Baby** in the barbershop, crowded, as usual, checking to see if Mr. Carter had repaired the soles on my imitation Nettleton shoes, then made a pit stop across the street to Rose's five & dime for some Squirrel nuts. After crossing Goff Street and speaking to Miss Annie in front of her fish market, sweeping, I dropped my school pants off at Mr. Curtis to be cleaned and pressed. Along the way, I saw the regulars, *"Itchy Brother"* and, of course, *"Wild Bill,"* swaggering down Church Street wearing his cowboy hat and boots, packing his two-toy gun holster. *As usual, they were in rare form!* At the steps of Daddy Grace's Church, I hid my money in my socks between Princess Anne Road and Virginia Beach Blvd. It could get dicey if none of the fellas I knew weren't around if you get my drift. I was in luck if Frog, Dip, Mummy ('Lil Fil'), or Blue Jack were shining shoes at the parlor across from Toy Sun.

On a typical Saturday morning, business would be booming! The beer gardens or taverns, reeking of stale beer, were opening, and stocking Pabst Blue Ribbon, Regent, Schaeffer beer, and Champale. At the same time, the music of the Sidewinders, the Showmen, Ruth Brown, and Gary Bonds saturated the atmosphere. There was never a time I was not mesmerized by Church Street and all the happenings, from seeing the Showmen in their processes hanging out at Frankie's Birdland, especially Norman Johnson, who lived down the street from me on Washington Avenue. Also, I loved looking for what was *"coming soon"* at the Regal, Carver, Lenox, or Dunbar theaters while inhaling an array of delightful odors like fresh peanuts from Regal's Peanuts, Mister Davis's hot apple and potato jacks, and the smell of fried crabs.

Normally, I would *'window shop'* and just *'daydream.'* But today, since I had money to spend, I bypassed the **Stark and Legum Men's Wear** and made a beeline to **Arthur's Men's Store**, where, instead of merely looking, I could actually walk in! I had my eye set on this beige and sky-blue Italian knit for weeks, and though I already knew what to buy, I decided to stop in **George's Fine Men's Shop** just for the heck of it, passing by Queens Lounge, a place I could not *wait* to hang out, until I was old enough.

First, of course, I perused **George's** windows and then slowly walked in after the Campostella bus let everybody out so I could be seen (ha-ha). If $20 for the $19.99 Italian knit wasn't burning my pockets, I would have ventured down to the downtown Plaza to **WRAP** to see Jack Holmes, **but not today!** Finally, with my Arthur's *'bag,'* I strolled back down Church Street, picked up two starched shirts from Sunlight Cleaners, learned out when my pants would be ready, got my Nettleton shoes from Mister Carter's Shoe Repair, and headed to Ed's Shoeshine parlor, one happy camper!

CHAPTER VII- WHAT IS *"The Norfolk We Remember?"*

Are you someone who *"does not do Facebook"* because *"you don't care"* to know if someone is currently eating at IHOP? Of you *"don't have time for Facebook."* You don't want people to know your *'personal'* business, or you just don't believe in social media? I am so excited to invite you on an adventure unlike any other!

To describe precisely *"THE NORFOLK WE REMEMBER"* is akin to an Almond Joy as *"Indescribably Delicious,"* created when a contest was conducted to come up with the best two words to sell this candy bar. *"THE NORFOLK WE REMEMBER"* is like the Lay's Potato Chips dare: *"Bet you can't eat just one!"* I double dare you to join us on Facebook. I guarantee you can bet your last money; it's all going to be a stone gas, honey. It would be unjust to label *"THE NORFOLK WE REMEMBER"* as just another Facebook page because it is multi-faceted, with various different and vital group dynamics.

The Norfolk We Remember is described as a melting pot where a variety of individuals from multiple locations and social-economic levels assimilate into an interconnected whole.

PICTURE THIS: There is this vast Facebook assembly of *"The Norfolk We Remember"* folks donned in pajamas, nightgowns, and slippers. Some are well into their 80s, from an era when electric typewriters and *"wite-out"* were technological advances. Now, they are maneuvering the keyboard of laptops and smartphones- an age group with a cache of *previous nuggets* stored in *their memory* hard drive. For instance, remember, as kids, how proud we felt when we first learned to spell gigantic words like *Mississippi* and *Encyclopedia.*

This generation of folks now has hair growing *everywhere* in our nose and in our ears*, but* not where we desire*, on our heads!* An age group that remembers when there was carbon copy paper long before *"copy and paste."* Folks can recall exactly where we were when hearing of the Kennedy assassination, as distinctly as *"9-11," but* for the life of us, we cannot remember why we just walked into the kitchen.

In my *"small world,"* I grew up ashamed that until the sixth grade, our home had no electricity, hot running water, and an outhouse. I thought only the *'well-to-do'* did not eat the end slices of loaf bread! While engaging in conversations on Facebook, *"The Norfolk We Remember,"* about iceboxes, oil lamps, and *'miss-ham'* sandwiches; I was shocked when someone else had similar childhood experiences.

VISUALIZE THIS! As teenagers in the segregated Tidewater area, we had finally graduated from junior high school. Some of us were from Jacox Junior High, some from Ruffner or Rosemont, and others from the, then, new Campostella Junior High School. All summer long, we anxiously anticipated that first-day walk or bus ride to Booker T. Washington High School, the *only* Black high school in Norfolk! The night before the first day as an official *'High Schooler,'* we went into the house earlier than usual, laid our *'school'* clothes out, bathed, and hit the sack! You worked summer jobs getting all your school clothes together, or like me, nervously waiting for Grandma to take me *"school shopping"* on Church Street or the Downtown Plaza.

In what seems like only minutes, startled, you are roused by the bellowing voice of Jack Holmes, **"Get Up Outta That Bed!"** For those like me, who walked to Jacox with friends, now we would still travel the same route, but we would eventually veer off to our *"New"* school. Upon entering our homeroom class there were many unfamiliar faces but seeing somebody we knew was comforting. In our new homerooms, we sat elbow to elbow with sons and daughters of professionals like doctors, funeral directors, teachers, and so on! I thought it cool learning that Mrs. C.F. Jones, my homeroom teacher's son Lawrence, was in my homeroom class.

For the next three years, we cheered for our **'Fighting Bookers"** on the cold football field and basketball team in the chilly gym we called **"The Dungeon."** Some of us became a Tau, an Omega, or marched and performed in the best band ever! Before we knew it, three years had zoomed by, we graduated, and we went our separate ways. Many of us were drafted or joined the military, enrolled, received college scholarships, or relocated, while many just began *'Life.'* The Booker T. Washington we attended was now just a memory as time elapsed.

The argument that integrated schooling was far better than segregated schooling is ongoing. While at Booker T, some of you, like me, may have yet to grasp the impact of attending a school with *all*-Black students, *all*-Black teachers, and *all*-Black administration. However, the notion that integration destroyed something uniquely valuable to Blacks in the South had been powerfully impacted by our memories of and about our Black teachers.

Black schools were places where obedience prevailed, where teachers commanded respect, and where parents supported the teachers. Teachers, pupils, and parents formed an organic community that treated schooling as a collective responsibility. In our neighborhoods, we knew a teacher or educator on almost every block. **What A Melting Pot!**

The phrase *"ALL ROADS LEAD TO ROME"* has its roots in the centralization and road building of the Roman Empire over 2,000 years ago, that spread from the city of Rome like the spokes of a wheel. At least, for Europe, it has been proven that *"All roads do lead to Rome,"* and that you can reach **Rome** on almost 500,000 different routes across Europe.

Throughout our lives, *'The Road'* has provided an excellent metaphor for our life's journey. With amazement, we can look back over the winding slopes of difficulty, the narrow pass of opportunity and the *choice* between security or chance. Also, *"All Roads Lead To Rome"* is proverbial, implying many diverse ways of achieving the same goal or result.

When our **Road** divided, we made the decision that led us, in this case, to *"The Norfolk We Remember."* As you continue your *"Road trip"* on *"The Norfolk We Remember,"* whether you are still working or retired, whether you are *"well-off"* or making it by the Grace of God, remember, it takes *ALL* of us to make a *Melting Pot Village.*

So, let us enjoy our daily Norfolk *"Back in The Day"* unique memories such as eating *'Norfolk-only'* favorites such as small smokes, combination sandwiches, hard-shell fried crabs, and *That's-A-Burgers*. Chinese noodles with a choice of meat, diced raw white onions, a ketchup and soy sauce broth, and a hard-boiled egg finished it off by sprinkling cayenne pepper over the top. Tell me, where else can you buy real *"Yock"*?

What ever happened to Carrols Burgers? Before McDonald's had Big Macs and Burger King had Whoppers, we had the burger chain Carrols where we got our fast-food meals at lunch time or after the night Booker T football games. Carrols Burgers was the burger joint of choice in its heyday! Hamburgers were 15 cents and milkshakes were 15 cents and French fries were a dime, so it was 40 cents for a meal.

Let us enjoy, again and again, those fun times hanging out at Booker T Drive-in or Carrols, recalling *"Our"* culture known as *la dolce vita (the sweet life).*

THE NORFOLK WE REMEMBER" IS A MAGNIFYING GLASS

While *magnification* is the process of enlarging the appearance, not the physical size, of something, such as visuals or images, *magnification* does not change the image's perspective. Therefore, to *magnify* implies having the ability or the power to cause objects to increase by their effect and size, appearing more significant than they are.

If all this mumbo-jumbo confuses you, maybe this illustration will explain it better: I remember, back in the day when marijuana smoking was *"copacetic,"* that before I rolled a *'joint,'* I made sure there were no seeds in it. You, Brothers who have not been saved all your life, might identify with this: Once, while out partying, gazing down at the private parts of my tan bellbottoms, was a tiny burnt hole from a popped seed. While I tried not to draw attention, I felt *EVERYBODY* saw it! I wasn't driving then, so here I was on a well-lit subway train, trying to conceal this tiny hole that seemed as big as a golf ball.

And Sisters, if you are like my wife, you might identify with this: You have been cleaning the house all day, preparing for a *'Girlfriend'* gathering. Even after they arrive, praising you on *"How clean and well-kept your house is,"* you *still* see areas that you missed vacuuming, dusting, or wiping! *A better example is the ballooning of *"The Norfolk We Remember,"* swelling from a handful to over hundreds of members.

There are two kinds of magnifying, microscope magnifying and telescope magnifying. The microscope makes a small thing look bigger than it is. The telescope makes a big thing look as big as it is. On our computer or cellphone, we have a *zoom control* that allows us to increase or decrease the size of a whole web page or all the text to improve readability. Instead of changing the size of everything, we can change the font size.

Likewise, *screened* memory is a recollection of our childhood that may be falsely recalled or magnified, in importance, that masks another memory of deep emotional significance. Someone once said, *"The heart's memory eliminates the bad and magnifies the good."* Giving lesser weight to negative memories or greater importance to positive memories is a type of *Magnification.* Our positive memories are embedded with all the sights, sounds, smells, sensations, feelings, the associated meaning of the events, and remembrances of a happier time.

We quickly remember the good times and readily forget the tough ones, all based on how and where memories are stored. We may require painful memories for emotional reinforcement, but we can also *amplify* or *remember* our good memories.

Likewise, under a magnifying glass, our feelings, memories, and senses are all *BIGGER* and *MORE ROBUST* when the memory rolls around. It is a like a pinball machine, our memories pinging and ponging. The more it pings and pongs, the stronger memories moves around in our minds. Suddenly, *we are revived!* To *Revive* means to come back or bring something back to life, health, or to a state of new energy. It is like a plant *revived* as soon as we give it some water. It's akin to a hot shower or cup of tea that *revives* us. Welcome to *"The Norfolk We Remember" Revival!*

After experiencing something new, the memory event is stored in various aspects of our memory, such as the *location* where the event occurred, or *emotions* associated with the memory. Think about that first surprise birthday party when someone entered with a cake. What was your facial expression? If you have a hard time imagining how you looked *then* rather than now, you are not alone. Our brain edits memories relentlessly, updating the past with current information, and it isn't a question of us having a bad memory. Our memories are not perfect, and they are not like tape recorders!

Do you *remember* your first childhood beach trip to City Beach, Buckroe Beach, Seaview Beach, or Sunset Lake Park? Can you *recall* the color of your bathing suit, the softness of the sand, or the excitement of your first swim in the ocean? Our early memories, such as these, often *revive* us via faded family pictures or archived Journal and Guide clippings. With time, memories lose their rich vividness, and memories can also become distorted as our life experiences tangle with a dimming past. Instead, the brain *updates* memories to make them relevant and sound, even if they are not an accurate representation of our history.

An Advertiser's most crucial challenge is not merely to attract our attention but to *get* our *focus* on their product. If an *'Advertisement'* will evoke a response that will last longer than a few seconds, it must cause a feeling related to the brand to be planted in our memories. The *'Ad'* must create a virtual *magnifying glass* highlighting something specific about the brand. Some facts, ideas, or impressions give us *enough* emotional charge to be planted in our memory: Welcome to *"The Norfolk We Remember"* Revival.

Our *'TODAY'* is molded not by our personal history but also by our mental visits to the past, like revisiting *"Hell Night"* in High School over half a century ago. *Or* reminiscing about an old *'Hopscotch'* or *'Marbles'* friend. *Or* cringe at the thought of our awkward adolescence on that *"first date"* asking a girl for a *"Chance."* You know *"that one,"* brothers!?!

That *one sister* we, brothers sang to: *"Each day through my window, I watch her as she passes by. I say to myself you're such a lucky guy. To have a girl like her is truly a dream come true, out of all the fellows in the world, she belongs to me."* When we lose pieces of the past, we lose pieces of our identity. Memories fade and transform as we age, having to do less with the age or content of a memory and more with what we *do* with that memory. Changing the past might be easier than we thought. Chances are, we do it each time we log into *"The Norfolk We Remember."*

THE NORFOLK WE REMEMBER" Is Watching A Family Video

Remember *'Back in the Day'* when after a day at work or on the weekend, we would say, *"Let us stay at home and watch a video!"* We stopped at Blockbusters or West Coast Video, picked up some goodies, took off our work attire, got comfy, dimmed the lights, and hit *"Play"* on the VCR. What would we see if our childhood had been videoed without knowing? *Glad You Asked!* Get your cup of hot brewed coffee or Green tea, grab the remote and kick off your raggedy but comfortable slippers- *the ones you have meant to throw away for years!* Now, flop down in your recliner or favorite spot on the couch.

As *'Your Childhood'* video began, surprisingly, there were no opening credits, just a familiar neighborhood scene where you played the game *"May I."* You fell and got your first knee scar trying to roller skate, learned to Double Dutch, and chased the *ice wagon* for a chunk of ice on a hot summer day. Immediately, you recognize the days when your neighborhood included family members, neighbors, preachers, teachers, police officers, politicians, and even the owners and employees of the local corner stores. Instantly, memories of an era when few on-the-block owned televisions *are rekindled.* You recall the joy of visiting that friend across the street who *had* a TV, sitting on the floor watching cartoons, *Red Ryder,* and Saturday college football games, often dozing off right there on the floor.

While reminiscing, you hit the *"Pause"* button, race to the bathroom, go to the bedroom for your meds, picking up a bottle of spring water on the way back to the tilt-back recliner. After hitting *"Play"* again, the scene switches, and you find that you are walking through various recognizable surroundings encountering other kids, some your age and some a few years older. They are all wearing tags around their necks with their names on them. In one scene, you are in the Rio theater watching *"The Blob,"* and as you scan the theater during intermission, you are amazed to see so many names of people you have met since joining *"The Norfolk We Remember"* on Facebook! The scene shifts to the Regal, where *"Jailhouse Rock"* is playing.

Waiting to get in, a line looped from the Regal theatre around Virginia Beach Boulevard to Wide Street. Walking to the end of the line, you are astonished at how many familiar **nametags** you recognized from interacting on Facebook with a *'comment'* or *'like'* on *"The Norfolk We Remember."*

Flabbergasted, you click the *"Pause"* again to take your high-pressure medication. After getting yourself together, you sit upright in the recliner instead of lying on the couch. As you hit *"Play"* again, there you are rubbing shoulders at the **Far East** during lunchtime at Booker T. You are shouting to place your **small smoke** and French fries order, but when you look behind and beside you, you see more Friends of *"The Norfolk We Remember!"* As you continue to watch *"Your Childhood"* video, you are at crowded Friday night football games on Booker T or Foreman Field. Games you could not miss for the world, whether you paid or hopped the fence. In the next scene, while standing in line for a *"That's-a-Burger,"* again, you see recurring name tags of *"The Norfolk We Remember"* friends sharing childhood experiences never to be replicated! As the video goes off, oddly, it doesn't say *"The End."* Now, it has become apparent that what you experienced was mystical.

Marketers use videos as the crucial performance indicator, **Recall**, to enhance a marketing campaign's influence because it has proven effective in generating an increase in brand, **Recall**, and the product's message. How many times a day did we *recall* hearing the following sayings, over and over, back in the day? *"Plop, plop, fizz, fizz"* ... *"It takes a licking and keeps on ticking"* ... *"Melts in your mouth, not in your hand"* ... *"Sometimes you feel like a nut, sometimes you don't!"*

"The Norfolk We Remember" is where those from Norfolk, now living in various States, share childhood experiences simultaneously in the same place and time. It is not luck; **You Can't Make This Snuff Up!** Nowadays, we can **stream** a video that sends the content in compressed form over the Internet, displayed by the viewer in real-time, and we do not have to wait to download a file to play it. Instead, the media is sent in a continuous stream of data and is played as it arrives. If the current *"Me"* could travel back to the 1950s and early 60s, would I love the **same** things I did as a teenager the first time around? **Absolutely!!** If I had a time machine, or if **Scotty could beam me up,** I would spend a weekend shopping at **Arthur's Men's Shop** on Church Street ... I would sit back in the glider on Grandma's porch at 1415 O'Keefe Street on a breezy summer night, enjoying a couple of Kelly's *'mobetter'* chili hotdogs and a Wood's Drug Store cherry coke while listening to the vibrant horns and booming drums of **The House of Prayer Revival**.

I wonder if ***nostalgia*** is some harmless urge to bring back long-forgotten times or a psychological need to preserve our identities as we get older and our memories fade, ***BUT*** I wouldn't trade it for silver or gold. It is akin to a ***Family Video*** comprised of whoever we choose to live with and spend our time with and it doesn't have to be because it is blood related. Therefore, since this video is amended daily, ***Smile, You are On Candid Camera!*** I considered it a blessing being a member of ***"The Norfolk We Remember"*** Family Video.

Significance is defined as having the quality of being ***"Significant,"*** meaningful, or necessary. It also refers to the meaning of a thing.

Significant implies too closely correlated with being attributed to ***chance***. In other words, are you not just reading this book, nor are you just a member of ***"The Norfolk We Remember"*** by accident?

Significance begins with ***sign*** for a reason. An event's ***significance*** is a ***sign*** of its importance. The ***Significance*** of something can be implicit or explicit, meaning it can be transparent or known with a deeper understanding of the situation.

What is the ***Significance*** of ***"The Norfolk We Remember"***? It is the multitude of us, who were often at the same place and at the same time during our childhood, never discerning how ***significant*** the moment was ***at that time.***

Hence, when on Facebook, ***The Norfolk We Remember,*** I concluded three things: **(1.)** ***We all spent a lot of time 'in the house' ...*** **(2.)** ***Television was family-centered and not just furniture and...*** **(3.)** If I didn't know better, it appears growing up: ***WE ALL SHARED THE SAME HOME!***

"THE NORFOLK WE REMEMBER" A COINCIDENCE? I DON'T THINK SO!

Coincidences have always sparked curiosity and fascination. Citing a coincidence is how we explain unexpected events and surprise meetings.

This Humorous Joke Is A Good Illustration: Four expectant fathers paced in a hospital waiting room while their wives were in labor. The nurse enters and tells the first man, *"Congratulations, you are the father of twins."* *"What a coincidence,"* the man replies. *"I work for the Minnesota Twins baseball team."* A little later, the nurse returns and tells the second man, *"You are the father of triplets."* He answers, *"That is an incredible coincidence! I work for the 3M Corporation."* An hour later, the nurse tells the third man that his wife has just given birth to quadruplets. The man says, *"I don't believe it! I work for the Four Seasons. What a coincidence."* After hearing this, everyone's attention turns to the fourth guy who has just fainted. He slowly regains consciousness and whispers, *"I should have never taken that job at Millennium Computers."*

Chance has been studied from many different perspectives that have been present since the beginning of life itself. Sometimes, everything synchronizes so that two seemingly unrelated situations match up. As a result, people have always associated these chance occurrences with a higher power, making us wonder if they are *Coincidences* or *Fate*. Why were we born? Why into this family, this country, these circumstances, and not others? Is there something that can explain it? We often label it as a *Coincidence* when the unlikely or unexpected happens.

For example, you are thinking about a friend you haven't seen in years when suddenly they phone or text you, or you run across their name on *"The Norfolk We Remember."* Or perhaps you connect with a stranger with the same interests as yours in the most wildly unlikely places, *"The Norfolk We Remember!"* Or maybe only just this morning, you were asking a friend whether or not they believed in *coincidences*. Then, you stumble across a comment on Facebook just *posted* on *"The Norfolk We Remember,"* addressing *coincidences*. While some may term it as *Fate*, others might term it as *Coincidence* because they cannot explain, with any clarity, how else the event could have occurred. These events, which we would have never expected or anticipated, have altered our life course. Did we describe *"The Norfolk We Remember?"*

Coincidence has nothing to do with *Fate* or *Destiny*. Yet, like there are over five million minutes in ten years, we have all applied the word *Coincidence* countless times in common jargon to explain an unexpected event.

The terms *'Fate'* and *'Destiny'* are closely related, and they are often believed to be synonyms. *'Fate'* usually refers to a power that predetermines and orders the course of events. Even though the two words are interchangeable, there is little distinct significance in how they are applied. While the word *'Fate'* or *'Destiny'* cannot be explained, *Coincidence* is often used in mathematics and statistics terminology to describe a unique event or outcome.

The term *'Destiny'* is somewhat like the term ***destination.*** It is stated that ***destiny*** is a result, whereas ***Fate*** is the way to get there, referring to ordered, inevitable, or unavoidable events: ***It is what will happen!*** On the other hand, ***Destiny*** is depicted as the *'Finality of events.'*

Destiny and Fate refer to a future with a predetermined course of events that can't be avoided. In other words, *"The Norfolk We Remember"* was not birthed on Facebook but was ***destined*** over fifty years ago in a vision to this young Black girl named Kathleen in a small, segregated section of Norfolk.

Have you ever met someone one day and bumped into them ***randomly*** the following day or soon after that? Or have you ever read an article that answers a question you have just been seeking?

These seemingly random encounters appear to be *"signs"* of something ***significant*** is at work. When we state, *"There are no coincidences"* or *"It was meant to be,"* we feel fully confident in its truth.

The word *Coincidence,* mentioned only once in the Bible, is translated as what occurs by God's providential arrangement of our circumstances. In Luke 10:31, Jesus declares, ***"And by a coincidence a certain priest was going down in that way, and having seen him, he passed over on the opposite side."*** Jesus tells the story of a Samaritan man who was robbed by thieves, stripped of his clothes, and left half dead.

It was not ***by chance*** that the priest was on the same road: ***"He had compassion. So, he went to him and bandaged his wounds, pouring on oil and wine; and he set him on his own animal, brought him to an inn, and took care of him."*** Our God is not a ***by-chance*** God but a very present God in our time of need or trouble.

There are no happenstance or random events! Therefore, every person, every photo, every experience, and memory have all been assimilated into a portion of our destiny called *"The Norfolk We Remember."*

"The Norfolk We Remember," initially had only one member, Kathleen. Now, look from whence we have come! ***Coincidence? I Don't Think So!***

* *"THE NORFOLK WE REMEMBER"* IS A FLASHBACK! *

A *Flashback* is a phenomenon in which an individual has a sudden, usually powerful, re-experiencing of a past occurrence or element of an experience. These experiences can be happy, sad, exciting, or other emotions. A *"Flashback"* is applied mainly when a memory is recalled unwillingly or when it is so intense that the person *"relives"* the experience, unable to fully recognize it as a memory, not something happening in ***real-time***.

Enjoy Your Flashback! *Flashbacks* are memories of past experiences that may take the form of pictures, sounds, smells, body sensations, good feelings, or grieving moments. For example, it is common in cinemas for a *Flashback* that gives us a peep into the characters when they were younger, or the main character had done something previously. This *Flashback* was applied to help the viewer better understand the ***present*** situation. When we ***comfort*** someone on this Facebook site experiencing a *Flashback* due to the loss of a loved one, or when a photo reminds someone of a place in time that leaves them distraught, this is the heart of *"The Norfolk We Remember."*

I ***thank*** God for our various journeys on *"The Norfolk We Remember!"* Many of us have lived our entire lives in the Tidewater area.

Some of us left as children or adults and returned later in life; some left as children or adults and revisited so often it is as if we never left Norfolk; ***Some*** of us left and only returned to visit family and friends for special occasions, funerals, or home-goings. I am in the category that left Norfolk voluntarily at eighteen. I can count the times I have returned to Norfolk on my hands, only returning for funerals and the few Booker Washington Class Reunions I have attended.

If I had one reason to visit Norfolk more often, it would have been to see my beloved and strict Grandmother, the late Julia Towns, more than any person on this earth, who taught me precious foresight, such as *"Make sure you always wear clean underwear, in case you get hit by a car."*

Although I had been nurtured by the finest teachers from the John T West Elementary School through Booker T Washington High School, along with the wisdom of elders, my vision of a future in Huntersville was limited by the closed segregated community. A place where, for me, living to reach twenty-one years of age seemed an impossibility. For the *"The Norfolk We Remember Flashbacks,"* sharing familiar places and re-tracing the footsteps of a past I spent only a quarter part of my life, *I Thank You All!*

Since some of you are aware of a portion of my life's testimony from *"The War Within The War"* and *'The Sojourn From A Black Man To A Godly Man,'* you will better understand what I am sharing.

The feedback I often receive is *"When are you going to write your next book?"* or *"When are you going to write the next chapter of your life?"* Hindsight being twenty-twenty, that portion of my journey was *only* transcribed by me, but the *Holy Spirit* dictated it. Over the years, I have learned that our life experiences consist of *disconnected* dots, which through time, evolve into *connecting* dots. It is a temporary journey of revolving dots that is not complete until *all* the dots connect.

Let me make it more transparent: At eighteen years old, I joined the Army, not because I felt it was my patriotic duty, but to *get away* from what felt like a caged and limited environment-*Huntersville*.

Now, approaching seventy-three years old, I know, without a doubt, that *"all the days of my life were prepared before I had even lived one day,"* including the Facebook group dot, *"The Norfolk We Remember."* It was predestined that Kathleen would be an instrument by God *for such a time as this.* She utilized her *"Gift"* to research a fascination cultivated as a little girl while hanging out in the public library for hours and hours. We were ordained to be connected to *"The Norfolk We Remember!"* I did not just *leave* Norfolk; I *ran* from Norfolk! Now, daily I would sprint downstairs to my computer with anxious expectations for the daily *"The Norfolk We Remember"* Flashback.

As I continued to read daily the array of *'Comments'* of familiar places, re-tracing the footsteps of a Norfolk I spent the first 18 years of my life, here are some things that I found *unique* about *"The Norfolk We Remember:"*

I Am Amazed that growing up with camouflaged low self-esteem until I was eleven years old, our home had no electricity, no hot running water, and an outhouse. Then, while I engaged in conversations about slop buckets, iceboxes, and oil lamps with others from Norfolk, I was *amazed* to learn some of them had similar experiences growing up.

Through the assorted *The Norfolk We Remember* conversations; I discovered that I was not the only child who missed a meal or two! *I Am Amazed* at how my mother struggled with raising a slew of kids and how a grandmother who labored as a housekeeper for a white family found a way *always* to feed us. Though I remember going to bed hungry a few times, mostly because I *refused* to eat neckbone soup, pigtails, or pigs' feet.

*****I Am Amazed*** remembering countless mornings while on the way to school with no bag lunch nor *'hot plate'* money, finding a pop bottle or two that was good enough for six cents worth of those *'three for a penny'* cookies, along with a couple of **squirrel nuts** and a **Mary Jane**. Then, while reading a **"*comment*"** on **"The Norfolk We Remember"** from someone who also attended **"The Factory,"** they would recount a **many of day** sitting on the **Hungry Steps**, imagining the taste of a piping hot Mister Davis sweet potato puff. And like me, we knew what a **"wish sandwich"** was! We have come a long, long, way!

*****I Am Amazed*** when I revisit my **memory tour** school days from John T. West through Booker T, from the first grade to high school graduation. What I lacked in hope and economically, the Lord always placed me in homerooms where I sat elbow to elbow with the sons and daughters of professionals like doctors, funeral directors, teachers, and so on.

*****I Am Amazed*** when, on Facebook, **The Norfolk We Remember** posted photos of area events in Norfolk I recalled or attended as a kid, such as the Daddy Grace parades on the 4th of July, anxiously awaiting the Mighty Bookers marching band to pass or standing in the long line outside the Moton to see **The 7th Voyage of Sinbad** ... Enjoying such treats as small smokes from Frisco's or Toy Sun, and 15 cent pineapple sherbets from **High's Ice Cream Parlor** ... The thrill of relishing a snowball with ice cream at the bottom ... The awe of Black legends like Fats Domino, pulling up in buses outside the **Plaza Hotel** ... Watching boys and girls skating with colorful handkerchiefs or scarves fluttering from various neighborhoods in Norfolk *'noting'* in rhythm passing by my house on O'Keefe Street, bounded for a day of good clean fun on **C Avenue**. Before long, folks on **The Norfolk We Remember** would relate their **personal moments** skating on **Olney Road** or **C Avenue**.

I may have previously mentioned on Facebook some of these childhood memories. Yet, I am taken aback when someone speaks of a distinctive memory that I had carried for over 40 years, believing; **only me alone** still remembered *that* moment! Even though we may not have known each other back then, we were often in the **same** place at the **same** time! I am ***Amazed*** to be a part of **"The Norfolk We Remember."**

When someone walks through the cemetery, this is what they see, but what they will not see is what occurred between the dash. Our tombstones will be etched when we are born and die, for example, from September 23, 1949-April 5, 2029. In other words, your next chapter is right ***Now*** my **"The Norfolk We Remember"** family. **"You Are In The Book!"**

CHAPTER VIII- *WHAT DO WE REMEMBER MOST?*

Memory is fascinating because sometimes we forget what we want to remember. Sometimes we remember what we want to forget, and sometimes we remember events that never happened or never happened the way we remember them. Our memory involves a collection of systems that enable us to recall the past and imagine the future. It has been proven that when someone recalls an old memory, a representation of the entire event is instantaneously reactivated in the brain, often including the people, location, smells, music, and other trivia.

We work, play, and care for those pesky things like shopping and paying bills that are a part of everyday living. Sometimes, we want to forget about all that and relax. Recalling old memories can have a cinematic quality and often seem to play out in the mind's eye like an old movie. So, we look for entertainment to take us away from the everyday world into a fantasy world of ourselves. That might mean reading a book, going to a concert, listening to easy-on-the-ear music, taking a walk, going for a swim or to the fitness gym, watching a movie, or logging into *"The Norfolk We Remember."*

When I watch the oldies on TCM, which I do virtually every day, the first thing I look for is the date of the movie. If the date was 1959, I am reminded of those days when I lived in Huntersville, on Washington Avenue, for ten years. If watching *"Guess Who's Coming to Dinner,"* produced in 1967, I find myself in the Army six months after graduating from Booker T, in a segregated theater in Columbia, South Carolina. And I will never forget Christmas, *"The Wizard of Oz* shouting, along with the Munchkins, *"Follow the yellow brick road! Follow the yellow brick road!"*

My daughter and grandson cannot understand what I see in watching old cowboy movies or *"boring"* black and white TV movies. They are puzzled how the absence of color can be *"ALL That"!* I tell them you had to be lived during my time to understand. It's hard to explain to them that the dated look of the films is an image of time, like the varnish on old paintings. If I were to let them view some of the posts on *"The Norfolk We Remember,"* they would probably still be bewildered. Some folks rely on the *"Doctor Phils"* of the world when seeking tranquility; I prefer *TCM*, Turner Classic Movies, where I find a swift transit to sweet memories.

TCM is commercial-free, uncut, lovingly, and smartly presented movies running 24/7. The first movie ever to air on TCM was *"Gone with the Wind"* (1939), which has been shown more than 35 times. The most frequently aired movie on TCM is *"Casablanca"* (1942), which has been played more than 125 times. ***How Many Times Have You Seen It?***

Movies can bring back some of the best memories and even ignite conversations while watching old black-and-white films, westerns, musicals, or other genres. If we did not have **On Demand**, couldn't hit **Pause** to go the restroom to run a few errands or take a snack break, it would be as if we were sitting in the Moton, Lenox, Regal, Carver, Rio, Dunbar, South Drive-In, or some other neighborhood theaters. Those **Back in the Day** flicks makes for great memories. The story, the actors, or even the person who watched the movie with us can be why a specific flick sticks in our memory. When Seniors with Alzheimer's watch a favorite movie or television show, it can stir positive memories and inspire good feelings about the caregivers and loved ones.

There is an eerie correlation between old TCM films and *"The Norfolk We Remember."* Both are time capsules that preserve a unique period and collected memories that extend a lifetime. What is suggested, repeatedly, watching old flicks on the TCM and *"re-posts"* on *"The Norfolk We Remember"* is a kind of spiritual quest. It is a quest beyond or above the range of everyday experiences.

Take, for instance, the 1958 movie *"Vertigo,"* one of the great films about memory's dangerous fascination. This detective, haunted by a succession of failures, makes an idol of his memory, imprisoned by the past. His dark obsession gives birth to one of cinema's most unsettling love stories: a love affair between a man and the image of the dead woman he is determined to recreate.

*Memories can haunt and hurt, but also bring fulfillment, hope, and peace. If we must live in the present, our reaction to it takes shape from the memories and dreams we have acquired.

A movie I saw at the Carver when I was 13 years old was about a man who travels across the country to a frontier town for the funeral of a local rancher to share a recollection of *"THE MAN WHO SHOT LIBERTY VALANCE."*

It concludes with the famous closing statement: *"When the Legend becomes fact, print the Legend,"* illustrating how necessary our memories are to *SHARE.*

*Our stories are stories of a Legend! Each of us has a life story based on our individual experiences or autobiographical memories that *define* us and make *us unique*.

As we *SHARE* our life stories, we reconstruct a personal narrative, much like a memoir or screenwriter.

*The Following Story Is *Why Oldies, But Goodies Are Good To Revisit!*

A man recalls an evening when his mother was ill in bed and very fragile. The room was lit by only the flickering glow of a black-and-white movie on Turner Classic Movies. Suddenly, his mother recognized and was revived by Eve Arden's voice, the star of *"Our Miss Brooks."* She gently smiled. It was a small cognitive resurrection. Never mind that her son had little patience for Eve Arden and her compulsive wisecracking and her tedious insistence upon having the last word. The sound of that mundane voice restored his mother to the rich world in which there were Eve Arden movies. For a few moments, her memory successfully challenged the oppression of her condition. She was, however, inarticulately delighted.

So, you see, there is a method to our madness when we post old, fainted photos of our childhood on *"The Norfolk We Remember,"* in the same way as elementary school class pictures, old funny books, candy bars, and old TV shows. It is akin to taking prescribed medicine or mental therapy! *"The Norfolk We Remember,"* like watching old TCM movies, is our escapism. Not from our present *"now"* but an escape to a world of *"Who Remembers This?"* It is our corner of the universe where we can escape to a laugh, a *"pick me up,"* a *"Wow,"* or *that sing* from *"Norfolk Music We Remember"* that soothes us when life appears challenging or uninspiring.

Daily, life boils down to our experiences. We have had good experiences and bad experiences, but each of us is a culmination of the things we have done and learned. Memories are the treasure we keep locked deep within the storehouse of our souls to keep our hearts warm when we are lonely. Each of us has unique memories, unlike any other, that are constantly changing and being rewritten, reconstructed, and even discarded from the moment we are born until we die. It is essential to keep our memories around so that we can enjoy them. One thing I have learned in *"The Norfolk We Remember"* is the importance of sharing our memories. It is not just **commenting** but knowing that what we share will be read by others in a public way, and perhaps someone else might be inspired or aided by our *'Back in the Day'* memory.

One of the methods of keeping our precious memories *forever* is by imparting stories, a tradition that is as old as history itself. For generations, the family elders told stories to preserve the history of today's generation. That was the *only* way they could until someone invented writing. **Moments** we spent listening to Grandma as she cleaned the chitlins, snapped string beans, or cut potatoes. **Hours** hanging with Grandpa as he imparted, *"handed down"* wisdom to us while he re-painted the living room or tinkled with that old broken lawnmower.

These are priceless memories that remain forever young as we age! There is no telling how much history we know of because someone decided to write down what was going on in their lives. It is the reason *"I Know Why The Caged Bird Sings."*

Have you ever noticed how sharing an article or a photo allows you to relive those memories? It's because preserved memories are a pivotal part of all our lives. Old letters, photographs, scrapbooks, the family Bible, and many other things help us to recall our past and the history of our family and neighborhoods.

I have learned and experienced that sharing memories of the past draws us together! We strengthen shared connections, offer sympathy, and elicit support by telling a sad or difficult story, such as a fond memory of someone we have lost recently. Talking about the past also helps create and maintain our individual and shared identities. We know who we are because our memories provide a database of evidence for events we have experienced and what they mean to us. All these things, however, are subject to decay and eventual destruction if they are not kept current or *"SHARED."*

I was recalled being stirred by a *"The Norfolk We Remember"* post by someone from Norfolk, seeking to find anyone who remembered his deceased parents. Within hours numerous comments exploded on his post! I cannot even begin to imagine what this meant to him!

I encourage whoever reads this book to **share your story** because you never know whose life you might impact. Some of you, like myself, may not have any tangible memories such as old, fainted portraits or keepsakes handed down from generation to generation. Still, I have peerless memories forever etched in my soul and spirit that I would not trade for silver, gold, or riches untold.

The old television show, *"The Naked City,"* always concluded this: *"There are eight million stories in the Naked City. This story has been one of them."* I believe there are just as many stories and memories within us yet to be **SHARED**. If we do not share, it is not a story.

*May We Remember This: *Old things are more beautiful than many things brand new because they bring fond memories of things we used to do. Old photographs in albums and love letters tied with lace recapture those old feelings that new ones can't replace. The old things are more beautiful and more precious daily because they are the flowers that we planted yesterday.*

CHAPTER IX- "YOU HAD TO BE THERE TO TALK ABOUT IT" QUIZ

*An Excerpt from a Song by Janis Ian Remembering John F. Kennedy's Assassination titled, "GUESS YOU HAD TO BE THERE!" *

"Back in nineteen-sixty-three, we walked a fine line… We were taking it to the streets, skating on a thin dime… Love belonged to everyone, and we stood there singing "We Shall Overcome," knowing the eyes of the world were on us, Knowing the whole world cared… GUESS YOU HAD TO BE THERE. *In the summer of our youth, we came together, and we knew that our truth, it would live forever…We were going to make the whole world honest when a bullet got the bravest of us. Somehow nothing else was sacred, and we all stood naked. Now we listen to the news, and it seems all hope is gone, everybody feeling used, and there's nowhere left to run. Sometimes it seems like the memory is all that's left of our used-to-be. But what can never be denied is the way we changed inside."*

Some things you can't explain. A study discovered that people prefer hearing familiar stories to new ones, probably because people are generally such bad storytellers that brand-new tales are confusing. When we try to tell somebody about old black-and-white TV shows they have never seen, or record albums they have never heard of, we usually find them bored, confused, and underwhelmed. That is because our **'Back in the Day'** experiences are so matchless that they're nearly impossible for us to communicate well It's just not the same, *"You Had To Be There!"*

I believe in remembering because it allows me to tell myself different stories. I have many memories of my Grandma's living room: Putting 500 pieces puzzles together on the floor, watching **What's My Line? Amos 'n' Andy,** and **The Ed Sullivan Show**, every Sunday night. I realized that those extraordinary memories growing up in her house were moments that I *NEEDED TO REMEMBER!* Sometimes, in my spirit, I cry out the lyrics penned by the late Andraé Crouch, *"Take me back, take me back dear Lord to the place where I first received … Take me back, take me back dear Lord!"* We need to look back. We need to mark where we have come from and where we are going. Yes, there were some days when we doubted everything, felt nothing was happening, no one cared, and nothing was changing! With every step, we carried the possibility that we wouldn't make it. The **bigger** the hope, the **deeper** our desire, and the **heavier** the weight. Yet, in the midst, we must take a moment and perceive differently, look back along the path we have walked, and see how far we have come.

While the landscape ahead is primarily unknown, we can look ***Back in the day***, realizing that we have lived long enough to ***still*** share kindred conversations with folks from ***"Our Generation."*** Oh, how difficult it is for the younger generations to grasp our priceless memories photographically! ***"They had to be there TO TALK ABOUT IT!"***

When was the last time we got off our couch and went to a theatre to watch a movie? Or a play or a concert? Sure, it is fun to see things in person, but at the end of a long day, ***On Demand*** is streaming, and the couch is only two feet away. Yet, there's nothing like being there! ***"YOU HAD TO BE THERE"*** is applied when people cannot understand something because they did not experience it or see it themselves.

We have all had that hilarious experience that is never funny when we try to tell it to other people, right? ***"You Had To Be There,"*** we say, as an excuse for our lack of eloquence. But we don't believe it's our fault! There are simply some very funny moments that are ***only*** hilarious if they were ***There.*** It is like trying to tell someone about your experience at a live Richard Pryor show. Likewise, we often discover that our best reading experiences allow us to be so completely immersed in a story that it feels as though we are right there watching it all happen, not just having it divulged to us. For me, it was reading the Mickey Spillane ***'Mike Hammer'*** novels at the Blyden Branch Library on Princess Anne Road.

Sometimes, we have difficulty recounting a specific scene to our friends, as though it is their fault! We ended up saying, ***"You had to be there!"*** Imagine yourself at a Friday night house party where everyone is sweating, bopping, and living in the moment. That's what this is, ***a moment!***

Like those we got in school, a ***Pop Quiz*** is a short test given to students without any prior warning. ***But don't get nervous.*** If necessary, take your medication, knock off the cobwebs in your head, dust off your memory bank, and ***relax!*** Lame excuses like, ***"My memory's not as sharp as it used to be"*** or ***"My memory's not as sharp as it used to be,"*** will not be acceptable! After all, your brain is the most impressive organ in your body. It worked 24 hours a day, seven days a week, 365 days a year, from birth until the day you fell ***'in love.'***

Oh, and don't worry, there are no complex queries like the ***Question***: Where do you find a dog with no legs? The ***Answer***: Right where you left him. Or ***Question***: What do you get from a pampered cow? The ***Answer***: Spoiled milk. Also, there is no Fail or Pass. Before you start the test, I have a question that I have always been curious about: ***"Why was there a South Norfolk and not a North Norfolk?"*** Just asking!

THE *"You Had To Be There"* PREREQUISITES ARE: (1) Being a Grandma or Grandpop with Elizabeth River in your veins automatically qualifies you... (2) When you fall, you wonder what else you can do while you are down there... (3) You feel like you really hung one on the night before you realize you were in bed *asleep* by eight o'clock... (4) You get breathless playing chess... (5) The best part of your day is when your alarm goes off.

If you were bred or raised in Norfolk, just answering, *"Wow, I remember that"* would suffice. There is only one stipulation, no hear-say is allowed; *You Had To Be There To Talk About It!*

1. Do you remember playing the marbles games *'Baltimore,'* when many a child with dirty knees like you squatted to knuckle down with your *'cat eyes'* shooter on the edge of a large drawn dirt circle? In the middle was a bunch of small marbles. It is your *"turn'*, so with your shooter in your small hand, excited, you watch as the marbles scatter. If you were a good shooter, *"Richmond,"* triangular in shape, was the game! Today, marble games have faded out with the popularity of electronic toys and video games. You do not see children playing with marbles anymore. But you can remember when the magic of marble games captivated many boys and girls in the neighborhood because *You Were There To Talk About It!*

2. Growing up, did you ever spend hours and hours at Barraud Park, the first recreational area for Blacks in Norfolk? Before Six Flags and Great Adventure, Barraud Park was the Mecca center for pure children's fun, leisure activities, and various sports competitions. Barraud Park had a small zoo featuring *"Mike the Baboon,"* who would pee on you if you got too close. Barraud Park also had an amphitheater, basketball and tennis courts, football and baseball fields, and picnic areas. It was also the home of the legendary *Recreation Football League*, where the boys from all over Norfolk came to compete for bragging rights and hone their skills for, hopefully, a spot on the Fighting Bookers. Brothers, who remembers, after school, you and some of your homeys, high tailing it to Barraud Park, putting on football equipment for some good old football? I loved the Saturday games because there would be Midget league games all morning. Who recalls when guys lied about their age or name, praying Joe Austin wouldn't stop them from playing *'Rec Ball'*? I remember a classic Recreation Senior league football game, Browns vs. Saints, not decided for three days due to darkness: *the greatest sudden-death football game ever!* Who remembers watching our uncles, fathers, and *"older used-to-be"* baseball stars playing Rusty Dusty League softball games on musky summer nights under the lights? And who can forget those super competitive battles on the tennis courts?

3. Do you *Remember* those *'Back to School'* days when you used to enjoy covering your textbooks in brown paper bags at the start of each school year? How about shopping for new clothes on Church Street at Altschul's, Downtown Plaza, or L. Snyder's? Who shopped for shoes at the famous Coleman's Shoes Store? Do you recall when the first day of high school was all about logistics: Where's my locker? How early must I wake up to finish my paper route, get to school, go to my locker, and then go to my eight o'clock class *on time*? How many classes will I have before I returned to my locker to switch books? Where will I get lunch from, Kelly's, Mr. Allen's, The Far East, or the *'Truck'*?

4. Looking back, who *remembers* visiting or relocating to Redevelopment residences we called *"Parks"*? Now, Oakleaf Park is called Oakleaf Forrest, Roberts Park is called Roberts Village, Young's Park is called Young's Terrace, Bowling Park is called Bowling Green, Calvert Park is called Calvert Square, Moton Park is called Moton Circle, and Diggs Park is now Diggs Town. Even East Ghent became Ghent Square- *Go figure!*

"PARK" paints a picture of manicured lawns and multi-colored flower beds in a residential community of comfort, convenience, and the enjoyment of neighbors. The idea that you did not have to pack up and go to a *PARK*, but to live in one, was part of the attraction, I think. The *PARKS* even had their *own* elementary school and Recreation Center! Leaving O'Keefe Street to visit my friends, who lived in Young's Park, was like stepping into a new world. The terms, *Terrace, Village, Square,* or *Circle*, describes, to me, ritzy or bourgeoisie places, not a place where families lived, struggling day to day to preserve their portion of *"THE PARK."*

Finally, do you *remember* where you lived when Hurricane Hazel or Hurricane Donna raged through Norfolk? Were you living in the Tidewater area when the Norfolk-Portsmouth Bridge Tunnel or Chesapeake Bay Bridge Tunnel opened? Who remembers when parents took their children to John Marshall School to take high school admission tests required to determine placement in the white high schools in Norfolk? Do any of you *'Old Timers'* remember baseball games at High Rock Park (off Church Street)? Or when there were the *Norfolk Tars* before the *Norfolk Tides* or the *Norfolk Stars Negro* Baseball League team? Now, that wasn't so bad, was it? It makes you appreciate still being alive to talk about it, right? Moments when you wish you could roll back the clock and take all the sadness away, but you have the feeling that if you did, the joy would also be gone. Nothing lasts forever except the memories that are a part of us. Our memories make us, *US!* They are what we *have* experienced. *We are incomplete without them.*

***REMEMBER**: "A Memory Is A Photograph Taken By Our Heart To Make A Special Moment Last Forever."*

Among our abilities as human beings are the ability to think, know, and reason. Our knowledge may range from knowing people to understanding things. It may be practical and theoretical, covering the concrete and the abstract, the seen and the unseen. The word *"know"* reflects various skills and professional abilities to distinguish between good and evil, the wise and the foolish, the desirable and the undesirable, and life and death. The word *"know"* is also used to express an acquaintance with someone.

Knowledge is the apprehension of some fact or truth by its real nature. In a personal relationship, our intellect is connected to our affection and will, such as choice, love, and genuine caring. Knowledge is distinguished from opinion; *we know what we know!* Our intellect connects and reasons about these appearances and arrives at truths. Wow, that sounds like what is happening within the *"The Norfolk We Remember!"* Ever notice how enthusiastic the comments were when someone posted a historical article, especially about happenings in your *"old stomping grounds"* where you thought you *knew* everything and everybody!?! When I contemplated sharing this, the question, *"why knowledge now"* popped up.

In my latter years, after many life experiences, I can think of numerous things needed besides *more* knowledge! Then I envisioned thousands of senior citizens on smartphones, laptops, and desktop computers talking about everything from playing with Jacks, Bolo bats, Hopscotch and *Spin the Bottle*, to sitting with family, anxiously awaiting the next episode of *"The Fugitive."* It was then that it dawned on me that while our memory may not be what it once was, our mind is continually hungry for *knowledge* and the desire to possess and increase it.

Many of *"Our Generation"* were born before color television, penicillin, polio shots, frozen foods, Xerox, contact lenses, frisbees, and the *Pill.* Eating crabs and watermelon together made you sick, *so they said*. Many of us were born before dishwashers, clothes dryers, electric blankets, air conditioners, and drip-dry clothes, before man walked on the moon and when pregnant mothers ate laundry starch straight from the box. In *our* time, closets were for clothes, not for *"coming out of it,"* and having a meaningful relationship meant getting along with your cousins. We were before computer dating, dual careers, and computer marriages. We were before daycare centers, group therapy, and nursing homes. We only had AM radios and never heard of tape decks, electric typewriters, artificial hearts, word processors, yogurt, or boys wearing two earrings.

For us, *'time-sharing'* meant togetherness, not sharing the computer, vacation spots, or apartments; a *"chip"* meant a piece of wood; hardware meant *HARDWARE,* and software was not even a word! *"Made in Japan"* told us it was *junk,* and the term *"making out"* referred to a *D* grade on our final exam. In *our* day, cigarette smoking was fashionable. The *Grass* was mowed, not smoked, and *Coke* was a cold drink. You cooked food in a *Pot,* and *Rock Music* was a Grandma's lullaby. We slept on the porch in the summer because you did not have air conditioning.

We knew how to bisect a crab by taking out the *'dead man'* long before ever bisecting a frog in Biology class. Gas was only 25 cents per gallon, and you got good attendant service when you filled the tank. Headlight dimmers switch were on the floor, and radial tires were something new. Ice boxes had actual blocks of ice in them, we made lemonade from real lemons, and Coca-Cola was an elixir.

Today, our joints are more accurate meteorologists than the National Weather Service, and our investment in health insurance is *finally* beginning to pay off. We quit trying to hold our stomachs in, and no matter who walks into the room, our secrets are safe with our friends because they cannot remember them either! Yet, we would not trade our life journey for anything, right?

*"Our Generation "*was born and nurtured during a time of genuineness and respectability when revealed navels were only on oranges and Peyton Place was porn. Girls yearned for *"Cookie"* to lend them his comb... Guys rushed home after school to watch the Mickey Mouse Club because we had a crush on Annette Funicello. We danced to *"The Quarter to Three,"* sang to *"Tweddle-Dee,"* and *"Mama He Treats Your Daughter Mean"* by Ruth Brown, and cried when we lost Sam Cooke, Otis Redding, and Little Frankie Lymon. Only girls wore earrings at a time when three was one too many, and boys went to the Barbershop every other Saturday.

We had never heard of microwaves or telephones in cars. Babies might have been bottle-fed, but they were not grown in test tubes...*Microchips* were what was left at the bottom of the bag of Wise Potato Chips... Hardware was a box of nails, and *bytes* came from mosquitoes... Girl bathing suits were big enough to cover their cheeks, and skirts came to the knee.

And it was a great privilege to go out to dinner at a *restaurant* with our parents. Our memory was created as a time machine to take us back to a *Place* and *Time* where we fully appreciate how priceless our early days were. A place and time, *You Had To Be There To Talk About It!*

It is a known fact that segregation was never suitable for Black people or that we were *"not better off"* during Jim Crow. It used to pain me that there could be a positive to segregation, especially after reading the book *"Roots"* and later watching every episode on television. While we all know the cons, I will stick to the pros. For the most part, the Black dollar stayed in the Black community because back then, we didn't have a choice but to buy in Black neighborhoods. After all, the White communities would not allow us in their stores. Then desegregation came, which was a good thing, I think. Here is a humorous view on segregation: *"I sat in at a lunch counter for nine months. When they finally integrated, they didn't have what I wanted."*

There have been mixed messages about whether such efforts were worth the trouble. First, in 1954, there was the landmark Supreme Court ruling, Brown v. Board of Education, the decision to desegregate public schools. Norfolk had a Black side of town and a White side in the city; one Black High School and several White High Schools, *"two separate and unequal school systems."* Before integration, our Black teachers made do with hand-me-down textbooks, taught a limited curriculum, and worked in grossly inadequate school facilities.

Nevertheless, although Blacks now enjoy superior buildings, an expanded curriculum, and better equipment after integration, the overall quality of education has not improved at all. In the segregated school environment, teachers enjoyed close relationships with their pupils based on empathy with the individual student and intimate knowledge of the Black community. Integration destroyed that relationship by undermining the position of the teacher as a mentor, role model, and disciplinarian. It caused a loss of interest in learning for Black pupils.

Former Black teachers often questioned whether the benefits of *Brown* outweighed its cost by concluding, *"When they desegregated secondary schools in this parish, they threw the Blacks back a hundred years."* It makes me wonder, *Was segregation so bad?* The late Dick Gregory once stated, *"Segregation is not all bad. Have you ever heard of a collision where the people in the back of the bus got hurt?"* From the turn of the 20th century, Norfolk was a large Black professional community of Black-owned businesses, such as our own Black Hotel, *The Plaza* Black Newspaper, *The Journal and Guide*, numerous funeral homes, beauty salons, shoe repairers, lawyers, doctor offices and a variety of other professionals. We lived in a segregated world, a vibrant Black community with a thriving entertainment scene from the 1930s through the 1950s. We had our Churches, Community organizations, and music. Norfolk rivaled Harlem's culture, dubbed as *"The Harlem of the South."*

Also, we resided side by side on the same block, irrespective of family income level. And just as Harlem had detectives *"Gravedigger"* and *"Coffin Ed,"* we had Black detectives **Rambo** and **Christmas**. The civil rights era integration didn't bode well for America's historically Black neighborhoods. The segregation that brought people of different economic classes together began to transform during the civil rights era. Many of those who had the means, and the education began moving out of what had been historically Black neighborhoods. By the 1970s, neighborhood by neighborhood where we grew up had become desolate and unsafe. Black neighborhoods that once had been vibrant and, in a sense had disintegrated. Ironically, it is common knowledge African Americans have been and remain the most residentially segregated racial/ethnic group in the United States.

During the late 1950s, a white Naval officer from a small town in New Hampshire, assigned to the Norfolk Navy Base, seeking residence for his family in Norfolk, made this observation: *"In the neighborhood, I moved to known as Ghent, there were train tracks that divide the wealthier white neighborhoods, which were closer to the water and downtown shops. Far from the African American neighborhoods that were more inland and crowded with lower-income housing. There were certainly exceptions to this divide, but most of the residents on each side of the tracks were of one race."*

Today, sixty-eight years after the United States Supreme Court ruled that segregated schools violate the Constitution, public schools remain deeply segregated by race. We all think that integration is good but was the fight worth it? True, it's been a long battle, and we've had success. At the same time, we have many schools filled with kids of one race and background doing great. Norfolk's neighborhoods remain divided by race like many other cities. One study infers that we are more segregated today than we were 40 years ago, and Norfolk is still an extremely segregated city where white neighborhoods are between 80 and 95 percent white. Today, many of us are no longer inclined to live in the environment in which we grew up. We have increasingly become mainstream outside the Black community, mainly for safety and comfort. As a result, class segregation among Blacks has increased nor decreased.

Our matchless generation, which I will label, the *fossil* or *dinosaur generation*, was an epoch that will never be reproduced. When we were growing up, if we did something wrong, some lady down on the street would whip our behinds, then send us home. And by the time we got home, there was no use telling our parents that we had gotten a beating for no reason; we got another whipping, ***anyway!***

"Our Generation" grew up in neighborhoods when it was rare if someone died from a gunshot, and there was no such thing as a home invasion. The only items sold on our ***corner*** were sold at Harold's Market, and the only persons we feared after dark were the *'Boogie Man,' 'the Monkey Man,' 'Booty Bandit,* or the *'Corner Boys.'*

Back in the day, before the State Lotteries, we had our own neighborhood lottery businessman, Mr. Hank, the *'Numbers Man.'* He was a huge man who set up his *'office'* at Perkin's Grocery Store on the corner of Church Street and Lexington Avenue. Though not legit, it was widely tolerated. Hitting the number *'Big'* was parallel to winning the Powerball Jackpot. Playing a ***number*** was as much a part of daily life in the hood as shopping and working.

We grew up during an interval in time when we had neighborhood professionals like Doctor Buck, who delivered all my mother's nine children. I remember when we lived on Church Street, and she was *"due"* with my youngest brother. I recall running to get Dr. Buck, who lived on the corner of A Avenue and O'Keefe Street. ...I remember getting my gold crown tooth from Doctor James on Church Street. Also, I remember his sisters, both teachers at Booker T, who lived on Washington Avenue, down the street from where I lived. ...I remember how proud I was to attend Jacox Junior High School, named after David Gilbert Jacox, whose family lived two doors from my grandmother's house on the corner of O'Keefe Street and Johnson Avenue.

When we were children, we were surrounded by Black role models, and all our teachers were Black! Most of the guys I grew up and played sports with daily mimicked role models such as Jim Brown, Joe Louis, Willie (Say Hey) Mays, 'The Big O,' and Jackie Robinson, who was the reason I became a lifetime Dodger fan. I remember Mr. Jake Riddick, the owner of Riddick's Funeral Home, who lived on the other corner at Washington Avenue and O'Keefe Street.

Ironically, while poverty was an actuality, we didn't ***KNOW*** we were poor because we didn't have anything to measure it by. Many of our neighbors were at the same economic and income level, yet in our *"village,"* if we needed something, we could ask for or borrow it. Since only a few families owned a car, we would hop a ride, catch the bus, or walk to most places we wanted or needed to go ***Together!***

Most of all, Black people genuinely cared about one another. We lived during a time when we gathered on porches to talk when Black businesses conducted business among their own, and we made life as best we could.

When somebody died, folks in the neighborhood brought food and sat with the family. I never thought I would say this, but segregation wasn't all that bad! *Guess You Had To Be There To Talk About It.*

There's an ongoing debate about whether life was better in the *Good Old Days.* Many argue that those days weren't good but that we only *remembered* them that way. *Sure*, we grew up when there was a fear of Russians, evident by fallout shelters and drills in elementary school. *Sure*, there were some places we just knew were off-limits to us. My reply is, *yet we survived!* A considerable gap still exists between income and living standards, *so go figure.*

Whether the glass is half empty or half full is in the eyes of the beholder. For me, *"back when"* were better years because life was simpler. Kids spent time outside running around instead of sitting in front of computers and smartphones all day. There were fewer processed foods, and the family housing was tighter and in more significant numbers.

Life was not as complicated when we were growing up. Many television shows were about cowboys. The good guys wore white hats, and the bad guys wore black, so it was easy to tell them apart. The good guys never did terrible things, and the bad guys never did anything good. While to someone, it might sound insane to desire to go back to the *"Good Old Days"* of no electricity, out-houses, carrying pumped water, and iceboxes. *Yet, we had values back then,* valuing human interaction more than this generation. We also have memories that still linger, such as a double scoop of ice cream for 10 cents ... When we were young, we could go to the movies *alone...* A *Joint* was the wrong place to hang out and forbidden... We didn't know about toxic waste, the ozone layer, red dye, or cholesterol... *It was alright to give candy to children...* We rode our bikes *everywhere,* and never owned a bicycle lock, *but we did own a Union #5 skate key.* We never counted calories in desserts, and cream and butter were healthy ingredients.

So, what if there was no such thing as Automated Teller Machines? What if we needed cash and the banks were not open on *Sundays?* We just waited for Monday morning! Today, we have more *conveniences* and live in a hi-tech age. But then, we are in the Walmart Super Store *fast* check-out. There is this multi-tattooed, pierced nose and tongue of this smart-mouth Cashier with dyed purple hair. They are puzzled why we gave them $10.41 when what we bought only cost $7.41(??) ... We shake our heads and mutter, *"Give me the Good Ole Days, anytime!"*

What a journey, right? I pray that you took away something from reading about some of our growing-up days, whether in Norfolk or elsewhere. As children, we used to laugh hundreds of times a day, but as adults, life tends to be more serious, and laughter more infrequent.

Nothing works faster or more dependably to bring our mind and body back into balance than a ***Good Laugh***. Laughter is like medicine! Humor lightens our burdens, inspires hopes, connects us to others, and keeps us grounded, focused, and alert. It also helps us to release anger and be more forgiving. Best of all, this priceless medicine is fun and free! By seeking out more opportunities for humor and laughter, we can improve our emotional health, strengthen our relationships, find a happy place, and even add years to our life

I conclude our trip down ***Memory Lane*** with this: We have given many gifts to our children, grandchildren, nieces, nephews, and friends over the years. Some gifts will be simple, some extravagant, and most carefully chosen, and we will provide them more before our life is over. Some may be rare and unusual, the ***gift*** that makes the giver wait excitedly while the paper is unwrapped. But even those treasures could have been unwrapped by someone else. They are unusual but not unique! There is only ***one gift*** that can be given only by us, the ***one truly unique gift,*** our memories!

The gift of timeless memories, preserved in words and pictures, is an irreplaceable treasure ***only*** we can tell. It is a ***gift*** of our memories, captured, held, and passed on to others. Only we can maintain the timeless treasure of what we have lived, what we experienced, and what we have loved and learned. This treasure conveys our heart and our love most expressively; Even the treasures we made by hand, like that ***first*** school dress, or ***first*** milk crate skateboard, are but a silent testimony of our love for them. These things may add warmth and beauty to their lives, but, not even the most exquisite handmade treasure can't measure up the way ***WE*** can when we share the gift of our memories. Sometimes we must tell our story by telling ***our story.***

CHAPTER X- THE GRACE OF GOD

*"*MY REVELATION AFTER LEAVING NORFOLK*" **

Now, I would like to share the impact serving in the Army has had on molding me into the man I am today. Those of you who have read my book, **The War Within The War,** a large portion of my early experience growing up in Norfolk, are aware of this. When I enlisted, I had no idea what lay ahead, but I knew staying in Norfolk was not an option. Although I loved my Grandmother dearly, any hope of a future staying in Huntersville seemed unrealistic because *I had no aspirations or career ambitions.* In fact, as kids, my best friend Butch and I would sit under the 26th Street Bridge for hours, daydreaming. Our primary *aspiration* was to grow up *"Crab-men,"* catching and selling crabs!

So, when I enlisted into the Army on December 21, 1967, after that bus ride to Richmond, the day after New Year, I boarded a train to Fort Jackson, South Carolina. Sitting side by side on a train full of Whites and Blacks my age, felt strange. To say I was uncomfortable would be an understatement, yet before we arrived at the Fort Jackson Reception Station, I was on a first-name basis with several of them. I never looked *back* to where I had left, looking *forward* to what was ahead. I considered myself pretty smart, but it was not long before I received my *first* revelation. I had to go to the bathroom but could not find it, so I just followed the crowd until I saw this sign *"latrine!"* I had never heard or read this word and thought, *"Am I the only one that didn't know a latrine was a bathroom?!"*

During Basic and Advanced Individual Training, I received my *second* revelation that *not all white people were peckerwoods!* Growing up in segregation, for the most part, white people were the folks on the other side of town and always *"on the other side of the counter,"* so to speak. Now I was eating at the same table with white guys three times a day, sitting side by side in classrooms, sharing the same bathroom and shower, and getting drunk on 3.2 beer together. I even shared the same bunk bed with a white guy from Pittsburgh named Francis, who because my best friend. We even shared the same last name, Harris!

Stationed at Fort Jackson during these five months, we occasionally got weekend passes. A group of brothers would visit Allen or Benedict, two Black Colleges, to *"rap"* to some of the Sisters. Or we, Brothers, Puerto Ricans, and Whites, would go into downtown Columbia, where segregation was alive and well everywhere. It seemed as if *on-base* and *off-base* were two different worlds.

It was doing my time at Fort Jackson I experienced first-hand blatant hatred towards Blacks. Later, during my time in the Army, I encountered overt and covert racism. I had read the stories of Rosa Parks, Emmitt Till, the bombings in Birmingham, and the sit-ins, but at this stage of my life, if it did not *personally* affect my *space,* all was well. Besides, I had my issues.

On April 4, 1968, at Fort Jackson, when I received word that Martin Luther King had been killed, it reminded me of one Sunday when he visited a few years earlier New Calvary Baptist Church. I remembered how even during Sunday School class earlier that morning, Church was already half full, long before the 11:00 am Service: *I knew that something special must be happening.*

I remembered coming outside of Sunday School and seeing so many cars and people crowded along Wide Street and Virginia Beach Blvd. At the time, I recall being so glad when Grandma told me I could go home because the Church was already overcrowded. *It was like music to my ears!* Looking back, I realize what I missed was momentous! On this date, for the first time in my life, I *felt* pure hatred, and I was infuriated. All hell had broken out in Columbia, and the Platoon Sergeants were going around the various units to organize troops to go into town to serve as a deterrent to avoid destruction and possible deaths. The Brothers refused to volunteer. And for the first time in my life, I sensed a togetherness I had only read about-*Black Unity.* From that day, Francis and I realized our relationship had changed. Until honorably discharged, I witnessed openly prejudice and hidden unfairness, segregation, and an invisible *war within the war.* More significantly, I experience unmatched camaraderie, true brotherhood, and a Black Consciousness of Who I AM. *Oh, what a revelation!*

During my Army service, some moments are priceless that only brothers or sisters, who are Veterans, can identify. When I left Norfolk and made that long train ride to Fort Jackson, I was the only person I knew from Norfolk, but when I was at there, I ran into guys I grew up with: Herbert King, Julius *"Horse Collar"* Sessoms and *Lokie* from Galt Street. While stationed at Fort Dix, I recall bumping into Clemel Amlet, who I have known since John T. West Elementary School. While stationed in Korea, in the village, or *"Ville,"* I found myself hanging and partying with Joe Stovall from Lamberts Point, Michael Porter, and Jeffrey Banks, class of 66, many nights. When leaving Korea, I was at the Kimpo Airport, and the Air Force attendant at the counter was Alwin *"Do Boy"* Spence, BTW class of 67, who lived *next* door to me on Washington Avenue!

And while stationed in Vietnam, I crossed paths with *"Mingo,"* who I knew from the Lott Carey basketball court. *What Everlasting Memories!*

I recently watched a segment of the PBS documentary *"The Vietnam War"* that involved my time in Vietnam. Paralyzed, I revisited scenes of a blustering Saigon and all the activities that amazed me whenever I visited the city: *I never been to a city like Saigon!*

In Vietnam, I was already in the Army for three years, so I knew the *system* and how to get over it. Yet, now watching the *Truth* of what was happening, I began to feel I was just a little fish in an enormous aquarium. Me, slick *'Spider'* from Huntersville, thousands of miles from home, wheeling and dealing heroin, getting high, and partying in the clubs overflowing with girls who were my mine at my choosing!! It became clear as I watched the PBS documentary what was occurring in Vietnam and back in the States. That the *"The Establishment"* never meant for me or any *in-country* GIs to ever go home! It made me furious!

After the documentary concluded, I reflected on time spent in Long Binh Jail (LBJ), Leavenworth Military Prison, and decades of drug addiction. It became apparent that I was not in a grave in Vietnam or Calvary cemetery because of *God's Amazing Grace.* Not only am I alive, but when I left the military, I did not have only one Honorable Discharge, but *TWO!! WHAT GREAT GRACE!* God had a purpose for me in His Kingdom and had *"charged"* me to encourage, comfort, and bear the burden with others, especially the Vietnam-era Veterans: This is something I have done for over thirty-two years. *"Amazing Grace, How Sweet The Sound That Saved A Wretch Like Me!!"*

When I woke the following morning, this song, *"Silent Scream"* by the late Daryl Coley, dropped in my Spirit: *"Dressed up on the outside, things appearing well. Though you saw me through your natural eyes, some things you could not tell. But the One Who bore my pain fixed His eyes on the unseen, Jesus Christ, the Sovereign One, heard my Silent Scream. How He ministered to me because of what He saw. While others judged me from the outside, He beheld my shattered heart. He then rejoined my broken pieces, now with joy this song I sing, Jesus Christ, the Sovereign One, heard my Silent Scream. My voice echoed as if in the wilderness though millions gazed and passed me by, perceived complete and flawless, no one heard my cries inside. BUT there's One Who's always looking at the unnoticed behind the scenes, Jesus Christ, the Sovereign One, heard my Silent Scream. Now who you see is who I am because of what HE has done. I am encouraged to ask of Jesus Christ to point me to the ones who may be crying on the inside. Though unblemished they may seem, I'll point them to Jesus Christ, the Sovereign One, Who heard my Silent Scream."*

*"LIFE AND DEATH IS IN THE POWER OF THE TONGUE" *

An essential key to understanding the design of God's Word is through the meaning of Biblical numbers. 1 + 2 + 3 + 4 + 5 + 6 =**21**, which relates to the six days of the *COMPLETION* of God's Creation. When people reach the age of **21**, they are legally adults, recognized as having attained full maturity. Jesus Christ was twelve when He was first recorded as being about the business of His Father. Twenty-one years later, He fulfilled His *"earthly body and temple"* ministry when He gave up His life at thirty-three for us.

Growing up in Huntersville, as a kid and teenager, I was always haunted and tormented about not living long enough to reach twenty-one years of age. I saw it as impossible, especially since my mother died when I was only eleven. When I was discharged from the Army in Korea, a month before my 21st birthday on September 23rd, I returned to Norfolk, homeless. My grandmother passed in January, the home she raised me had been rented out, and asking somebody to take me in was not an option. *My pride wasn't having it!* Miss Elizabeth, our next-door neighbor, allowed me to stay with her until I *"got on my feet."* I signed up for unemployment compensation and completed numerous job applications. So, by September 17th I had re-enlisted and found myself on a Greyhound bus to Fort Dix, New Jersey, where I *celebrated* my 21st birthday, awaiting orders for Vietnam. I was on a plane to Fort Lewis, Washington, three days before Thanksgiving. Since I was an administrative specialist, I had requested special travel orders to spend my 30 days leave in Korea before leaving for Vietnam. Still, the orders received had me going to Nam the day after Thanksgiving, November 27, 1970. After I brought this error to the Personnel Officer's attention, my orders were revised, scratched from the flight, and I was to arrive in Vietnam after New Year's Day. Later that evening, word circulated that the plane I would have been on left McChord Air Force Base, stopping at Anchorage, Alaska. After refueling and a change of crew, the aircraft was bounded for Vietnam when forty Army and Air Force personnel were killed in a crash, which occurred while the plane was taking off in darkness and a freezing drizzle from the Anchorage Airport. I remember thinking: *Wow, I sure was lucky noticing the mistake in my assignment orders!*

Still alive at twenty-one, I found myself in a *"Hell"* called Long Binh Jail, or *'LBJ,'* scheduled to attend a General court-martial trial on September 17, 1971, the exactly one year from the day that I re-enlisted. Less than three hours after being sentenced to four years of hard labor at Leavenworth for the selling and possessing heroin, I overdosed on heroin and found myself in a hospital, where I learned I had been unconscious for three days.

I was informed by the doctors and chaplain in the hospital, I had just been pronounced dead at twenty-one, six days before my twenty-second birthday! *Lucky again,* I murmured.

On Thanksgiving Day, I was at Bien Hoa Airport, handcuffed and headed to Fort Leavenworth, when this loud mortar blast shook the entire airbase. I had been in Nam. for eleven months, stationed in the rear, so I had no clue what to do. I just did what everyone else did; I got on the floor until the coast was clear. All I could think about was, *"I get this close to getting out of this place, and now THIS!"* But when morning came, and I boarded the plane and was finally airborne, I counted my lucky stars.

Now Let Me Fast Forward: Working at the Philadelphia VA Regional Office, before retirement, one of my primary duties was verifying Veterans' PTSD claims for disability compensation. One of the documents at my disposal was de-classified records of mortar assaults during the Vietnam war. A frequent statement from a Veteran was his base receiving *"incoming"* mortar attacks, the cause of his present Post-Traumatic Stress Disorder. One day, I am attempting to connect this Veteran's claim of being exposed to *incoming* when stationed at Bien Hoa Airport Base. While researching this Veteran's claim, I came across the date, November 25, 1971, so I *Googled* the calendar for that date, and it was *Thanksgiving Day.* Thus, I could schedule the Veteran for a Veterans Administration PTSD examination since his PTSD stressor was verified.

It was then that God revealed to me that I had left Vietnam *precisely* one year to the day, November 25, 1971, when the airplane I would have been on crashed in Alaska.

God Revealed This To Me: The devil has been attempting to kill many of us from our youth, and while he cannot read our minds, Satan does shoot arrows of doubt, negative thoughts, fears of death, and suicidal tendencies into our minds and spirit that would manifest, unless God had His *own* plan for our lives. He told me that His perfect plan for my life could not be altered.

All I just mentioned was revealed to me *after* I trusted and *allowed* Him to take me on a childhood journey back to unpleasant and hurtful periods of my youth. The devil had planted this seed in me, as a kid, that I would not see 21 years of age, and I watered the seed by affirming *"living to see 21 years of age is impossible,"* but God's Word proclaims: *"LIFE AND DEATH ARE IN THE POWER OF THE TONGUE. I shall not die, but live, and declare the works of the LORD."*

ABOUT THE AUTHOR

Ronald Harris was born and raised in the Huntersville section of Norfolk, Virginia. He is a retired Department of Veterans Affairs Service Representative with over thirty-five years of serving the Philadelphia Veterans population. Also, he served in-country during the Vietnam War, and was a drug addict for over twenty-seven years. He and his wife of thirty-eight years, Ruby Dee, have two daughters, three grandsons, and two great-grandsons. Presently, he resides in Philadelphia, PA. He has served Jesus Christ, his Lord, ministering to incarcerated men in the Philadelphia Prison System for the past seventeen years. He is the author of seven other published books: *"The War Within The War,"* the story of a young, naïve Black soldier's inward military battles during the Vietnam era. *Norfolk Childhood Memoirs You Had To Be There To Talk About It* brings back remembrance of a priceless era, a place in time *back in the day*. *God Still Reigns Over Our Situations* is a journey through the "*Word of God,*" from Genesis to Revelation, that reveals no matter how many wrong life *choices* we have made, the option to *choose* Jesus Christ as Savior erases them all. *The Sojourn From A Black Man To A Godly Man* depicts and navigates the life journey of a young man as he struggles to replicate the love snatched from him when his mother died suddenly, early in his childhood. *Our Help Is From The Lord Who Made Heaven And Earth* that God Who, made heaven and earth, is greater than any life mountain situation. *"Remember, You Weren't Always Saved!"* reminds Christians that before God saved us, we *had no hope*, and were *without* God in this world. His latest book, *Are We Prepared To Re-enter God's Sanctuary,* is a revelation, an unveiling of sanctification on a purer level in the Body of Christ. While this book shines light on some uncomfortable areas in us, it is also perfecting those things that *please* our God.

Printed in the USA
CPSIA information can be obtained
at www.ICGtesting.com
LVHW040821190224
772223LV00004B/150